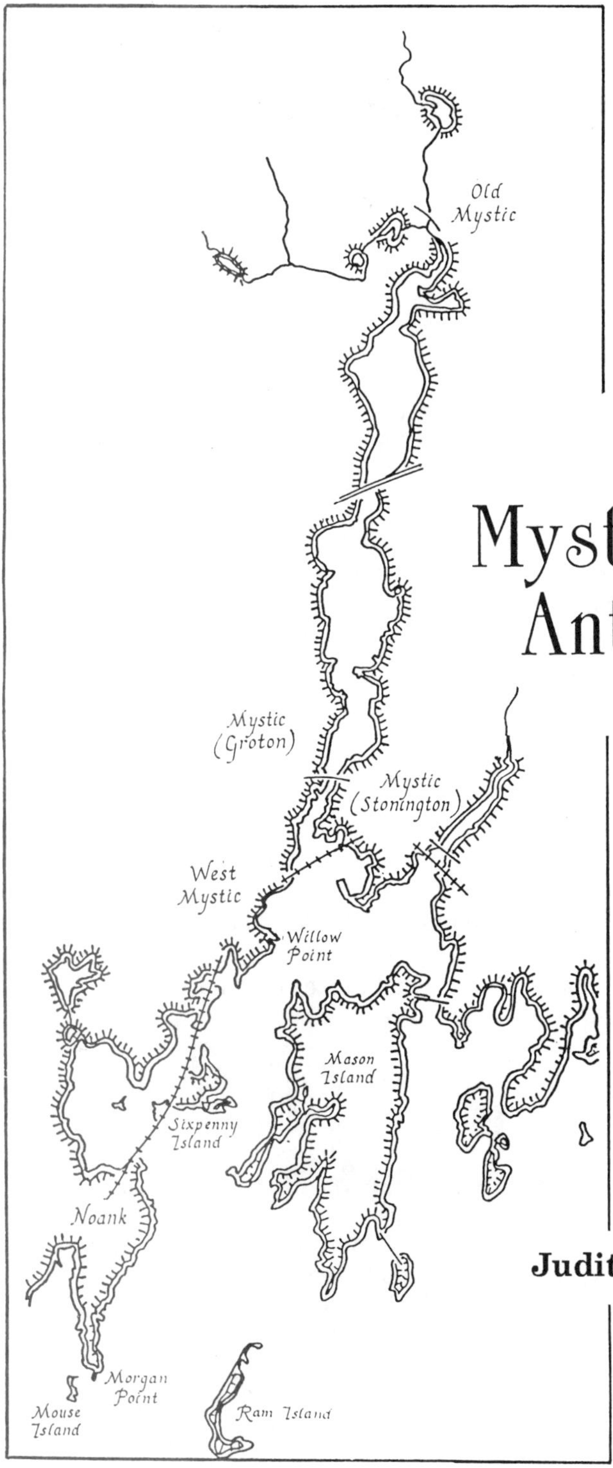

A Mystic River Anthology

Judith A. Hicks, Editor

A Mystic River Anthology

Judith A. Hicks, Editor

Dedicated to my many friends in Mystic

ISBN: 0-934881-03-0

Library of Congress Number: 88-071219
First edition: June 1988

Cover Design by John V. Cody

Printed in The United States of America

The Dutch Island Press
99 Brown Street
Wickford, Rhode Island
02852

Acknowledgements

Footnotes invariably detract from the smooth flow of reading. Thus, in this collection all text credits are indicated by a number enclosed in a box □ placed in the margin opposite the headline. Graphics credits are indicated by a single letter. Both boxed numbers and letters refer appropriately to the credit list below and on the following pages.

1. Reprinted courtesy of Mystic Seaport Museum, Inc.

1a. From *Maritime Mystic* by Virginia B. Anderson (1969), Publication #39 of The Marine Historical Association.

1b. From *Mystic: The Story of a Small New England Seaport* by Carl C. Cutler.

1c. From the folder *The Charles W. Morgan.*

1d. From *Guide to Mystic Seaport* (1985).

1e. From Mystic *Seaport Museum: What to See and Do.*

1f. From *Mystic Seaport Guide,* 3rd Edition (1952).

2. Reprinted courtesy of Mohegan Community College Bookstore and the author, Stan Gaby; from *Day Trips Through Connecticut.*

3. From *Connecticut Bicycle Rides* (1974), courtesy of the Connecticut Department of Environmental Protection.

4. From a composition book written by pupils at Portersville Academy about 1850. This poem by Lydia E. Burrows.

5. Various items from the *Mystic Press* newspaper.

5a. March 7, 1873

5b. March 15, 1888

5c. February 3, 1881

5d. March 3, 1881

5e. July 25, 1873

5f. March 28, 1873

5g. June 13, August 15, September 26, 1873

5h. April 24, 1874. Refers to Langworthy Hill murder five days earlier.

6. Reprinted courtesy of the author, Mary Cable, and Atheneum Press of Macmillan Publishing Co; from *The Blizzard of '88* (1987).

7. From *Seamanship* by S. B. Luce (1877), published by D. Van Nostrand Company, New York.

8. Reprinted courtesy of the Stonington Historical Society.

8a. From *The Stonington Chronology* 1649-1949.

8b. From "The Miser" by Charles Hyde Denison; *Historical Footnotes,* February, 1967.

8c. From "Remarks on board the ship Coriolanus of Mystic"; *Historical Footnotes,* May, 1978.

8d. From *Historical Footnotes,* August, 1970.

8e. From "The Packer Tar Soap Company" by Eleanor B. Read; *Historical Footnotes,* November, 1985.

8f. From "Mystic: Its Origin and Meaning" by Morse Allen; *Historical Footnotes,* November, 1963.

8g. From "Banking at Old Mystic" by Carol W. Kimball; *Historical Footnotes,* May, 1892.

8h. From "Elm Grove: A Cemetery in the Victorian Mode" by Marilyn J. Comrie; *Historical Footnotes*, May, 1981.

8i. From *Stonington Graveyards, A Guide* (a book).

8j. From "Mystic Island" by Eleanor B. Read; *Historical Footnotes*, May, 1984.

8k. From "Nehemiah Williams II, Stonington Planter"; *Historical Footnotes*, August, 1974.

9. From *A Wickford Anthology* and reprinted courtesy of Dutch Island Press.

10. Various items from the *Stonington Mirror* newspaper.

10a. From "The Liberty (?) Pole", July 11, 1872.

10b. From "Dewey Honored", September 29, 1899.

10c. Editorial, April 5, 1898.

10d. Letter to the Editor, May 12, 1899.

10e. May 3, 1898.

10f. *The Stonington Mirror-Journal*: From "Stonington, Mystic Dig Out from Disastrous Hurricane", September 23, 1938.

10g. Letter to the Editor, September, 1899.

11. From *A Wind to Shake the World* by Everett S. Allen and reprinted courtesy of the author and Little Brown and Co.

12. From *A History of West Mystic 1600-1985* by Kathleen Greenhalgh and reprinted courtesy of the author.

13. From an article in the *Mystic Pioneer* newspaper, March 19, 1859.

14. Reprinted courtesy of Carol W. Kimball, Groton's official Historian. (Other items written by Mrs. Kimball which are published in this Anthology are attributed to copyright holders Yankee, Inc., Stonington Historical Society, and the New London Day.)

14a. From *The Groton Story*.

14b. From *The Poquonnock Bridge Story*.

14c. From *A Brief History of Mystic*.

14d. From *A Brief Guide to Mystic*.

15. Reprinted courtesy of the New London *Day*.

15a. From "G & S, Last Mystic Trolley", February 27, 1986.

15b. From "Archaeologist to Search for Old Indian Fort" by Steven Rosenbush, January 13, 1987.

15c. From "Dissecting Squid — and liking it too" by John Matthiessen, March 30, 1988.

15d. From "Fashioning Home-Cooking Afloat" by Elaine Tait, May 31, 1987.

15e. From "Mystic, Noank Library: past, future" by Carol W. Kimball, November 19, 1987.

15f. From "Morgan Point: A Jewel by the Sea" By Barbara Reed-Collins, November 19, 1987.

15g. From "40,000 Throng Mystic Streets for 5th Annual Art Festival", August 13, 1962.

15h. From "At Red Brook Inn, a Ghostly Presence" by Susan Caronia, February 19, 1957.

15i. A letter to the Editor, July 2, 1986.

15j. From "Mystic Flagpole Topped off in 19th century Style" by Keith Phaneuf, March 26, 1988.

15k. From an article on November 20, 1986.

15l. From "Woodland with a colorful history rests now as peace sanctuary" by Steven Slosberg, February 20, 1978.

16. A printed handout (1987) to the congregation of the First Congregational Church of Mystic; reprinted courtesy of the author, Rev. Christopher Emerson.

17. From "Mystic Swing Bridge" (1981), reprinted courtesy of the Society for Industrial Archaeology.

18. From *Lights and Legends: A Historical Guide to Lighthouses of Long Island Sound, Fishers Island Sound and Block Island Sound* by Harlan Hamilton, published by Wescott Cove Publishing Co., Box 130, Stamford, CT 06904 and reprinted here with the publisher's permission.

19. Reprinted courtesy of *The Compass* newspaper.
19a. July 1, 1977
19b. From "Mystic's Worst Fire", December 16, 1960.

20. From *Drifting* by Stephen Jones; reprinted courtesy of the author and the Macmillan Publishing Co.

21. From *Shantymen and Shantyboys: Songs of the Sailor and Lumberman* by William M. Doerflinger; reprinted courtesy of the Macmillan Publishing Co.

22. From *The Black Ships: Rumrunners of Prohibition* by Everett S. Allen and reprinted courtesy of Little Brown & Co.

23. From *Noank: From the Papers of Claude M. Chester* (1970) and reprinted here courtesy of the Noank Historical Society.

24. From "The Pequot Indians" in the book *History of New London, Connecticut* by Richard A. Wheeler.

25. From *In Olde Connecticut* by Charles Burr Todd, The Grafton Press (1906); reissued by Singing Tree Press 1968.

26. From The Mystic Oral School 1975.

27. From Historical Study Sheets (1975) and reprinted courtesy of the Mystic Junior Women's Club.

28. From various periodicals (including *Seaword*) and publications of the Mystic Marinelife Aquarium, a division of Sea Research Foundation, Inc. and reprinted here through their courtesy.

29. From *World Book Encyclopedia* (1970), Volume 4 and reprinted courtesy of Field Enterprises Educational Corporation, Chicago.

30. From "A Time to Remember", Mystic Art Association, May 31-June 14, 1976; the material from this booklet is reprinted by permission of the Stone Ledge Art Gallery of Noank.

31. From *The Papers of Alla Lynne Perkins Allyn* and reprinted courtesy of both the Mystic River Historical Society and Cynthia Allyn Clapp.

32. From *The Mystic Garden Club 1924-1974* and reprinted here through the courtesy of the Mystic Garden Club.

33. From the column "Connecticut Crossroads" by Bill Rayn, January 4, 1987; reprinted courtesy of the *Hartford Courant*.

34. From the introduction by William Peterson to the 1987 Mystic House Tour program; reprinted courtesy of the Mystic River Historical Society and the author.

35. From *Mystic Walking Tour No. 1* (1976); reprinted courtesy of The Mystic Junior Women's Club and the Mystic Chamber of Commerce.

36. From *Village Fire Fighters 1883-1942* by Roscoe K. Burrows, printed by Stonington Publishing Co.; reprinted here through the courtesy of Briant W. Patterson.

37. From "Noank Notes" by Mary Virginia Morgan Goodman, April 8, 1981; reprinted courtesy of the *Norwich Bulletin* newspaper.

38. From "Mystic's Disastrous Dedication" by Carol W. Kimball and published in *Danger, Disaster and Horrid Deeds*; reprinted courtesy of Yankee Books.

39. From *Connecticut Outdoor Recreation Guide* (1976), Publication 46-A of the Connecticut Forest and Parks Association, Inc. and reprinted here through its courtesy.

40. From *A Cruising Guide to the New England Coast* (50th Anniversary Edition, 1987) by Roger F. Duncan and John P. Ware; reprinted here through the courtesy of Roger F. Duncan and Dodd Mead Co.

41. From *Voice of the Whalemen* by Stuart C. Sherman (1965) and reprinted courtesy of the Providence Public Library.

42. From *Mark Twain Himself* by Milton Meltzer; reprinted courtesy of Harper & Row Publishers, Inc.

43. From *Fieldbook of Natural History* by E. Laurence Palmer, 1949; courtesy of McGraw-Hill Book Co., Inc.

44. From *Major John Mason's Great Island* by James H. Allyn (1976); reprinted courtesy of the author and Roy N. Bohlander.

45. From *North by Northeast* by Ray Ellis and Walter Cronkite; reprinted courtesy of Oxmoor House, Inc. (1986).

46. From *Mystic Memories* by Eleanor B. Read and reprinted with her permission.

Graphics

Artwork

Cover design by John V. Cody.
Spot illustrations in text by John V. Cody.
Map by Martha Coffey; calligraphy by Melissa Hicks.
Marine drawings (L) from *Lore of Ships* and reprinted courtesy of Tre Tryckare AB and Nordbok, Gothenburg, Sweden,and Outlet Book Company, New York, 1985.
Marine drawings (S) from *Seamanship* (1877).
Whale stamps from *The Real Story of the Whaler* (1916).
Nawyaug House poster courtesy of Noank Historical Society.
Items in original type form from *Steele's Almanac* (1828) are marked T; and from *The New American Practical Navigator* (1832) are marked P.
Body sections of clipper ship hull from drawing by G. F. Campbell, A.M.I.N.A.

Photographs

Photographs not lettered in text are by Denice Walz, Anthology Photo Editor.

A Aerial photos of the valley by Edward David with airplane drivers Ralph J. Bradford, Jr. and Gregory Brown.
B Aerial photo of Mystic Marinelife Aquarium by George Cassidy
C Rick Turgeon
D Gordon Alexander of the *New London Day*
E Stephanie Gay of the *Providence Journal*
F Brooke Henderson, Mystic Marinelife Aquarium
G Cindy Pelloquin
H Robert F. Trier
I Paul A. Darling
J Photo of painting (artist: John F. Leavitt) of *David Crockett* by Mary Anne Stets and provided courtesy of Mystic Seaport Museum, Inc.
K Photo of $3 bill from a private collection and provided by Mystic Seaport Museum, Inc.
L James C. Burbank

H

Contents

MYSTIC

From the Editor:

This book is not a history of Mystic. Rather it is a collection of facts and events (and maybe some fancies) *within* the history of the Mystic Valley. There are articles, many of which have been written by local people, on Indians and ghosts, ships and trolleys, institutions and private homes, and robust community spirit. Taken as a whole, I hope they portray a bit of the flavor of Mystic... at least up into 1988. Taken individually, I hope they inform and entertain.

The production of this volume has become a personal expression of Mystic. I have lived in this village for over twenty-five years, brought up my three children here, and have been an active member of the community. Mystic is a place where it is just a natural thing to be active! Our volunteer projects, our churches, our Library, down on Main St., at the A&P - all places where a lot of projects have been born. By native standards I'm still a newcomer and in the past ten years many an out-of-towner has settled in - but back in 1847 a pupil at Portersville Academy was saying the same thing! Mystic is not a political entity (our zip codes and Fire District/Town taxes are most confusing) but it is a cohesive whole made up of all our people and activities from the headwaters to the mouth and along the banks of the Mystic River.

When I first contemplated this book I thought that I could put together in one volume the flavor of the yesterdays of the Mystic Valley. During the process of researching I found that it was impossible to include it all - the old and not so old newspapers, the many personal recollections, published articles, and texts are filled with interesting and revealing information. I have had to pick and choose and as a result have had to omit much. All my sources have been carefully acknowledged, however, and I urge the reader to seek out the original sources for more complete details. The Mystic & Noank Library has a wonderful collection of local writings housed in almost 100 year old beautiful oak and glass bookcases (the Library celebrates its Centennial in 1994) and the Mystic River Historical Society now has its many holdings under one roof in the new William A. Downes Archives Building on High Street next to Portersville Academy.

Reading about the many yesterdays provides one reason to ponder and smile. While *I* have not, Mystic has changed over the years - today commercial development has taken the place of the shipping and whaling industry, the recreation industry the place of the working of the land; but we still have our small-town incidents, we still have the feeling of "Mystic - our home town". It is this feeling that I have tried to convey with this collection. The selections, I hope, will make you think, smile, laugh and maybe want to read a second time.

Judith A. Hicks

....And the Publisher Who Learned a Lot

In a very real sense there is no river in Mystic, Connecticut. The body of water here *looks* like a river, is shown on navigation charts as a river, and for over three centuries has been considered a river. It's actually a long, narrow bay, a basin, if you will, into which empty a number of small streams from surrounding highlands. None of the streams carries the Mystic name, not even the principal creek at the bay's northernmost end, despite what the official Connecticut highway map calls it.

Understanding that we'd get some flak from those who, through long association with "the river", know better, we decided to trace that principal watercourse to its identifiable source, the true headwaters of "the river". We discovered long-abandoned Swantown, some seven crow-flown miles north northeast of Old Mystic and maybe three miles northwest of North Stonington Village, a very long way from the area covered by this book. There "the river" starts from a kettlehole as an east-flowing trickle which, growing in volume, eventually turns west as Lantern Hill Brook and south as Whitford (sometimes Whitford's) Brook before it reaches tidewater.

For the sake of this anthology, our peace of mind, and probably our personal safety, we've called it The Mystic River.

The proper adjective itself is a little misleading. Mystic as we know it in 1988 is not *a* village: it's two villages. One is to the west of the (non-existant?) river in the Town of Groton, not to be confused with the *City* of Groton which, so help me, Hannah, is part of the *Town*. The other Mystic is to the east of the river and is part of the Town of Stonington, not to be confused with North Stonington where (non-existent?) Swantown is.

Now that that's perfectly clear, we would be derelict in our explanatory - yea, obfuscatory - duty not to point out and clarify a few other irregularities we found; to wit, there's

—Olde (the 'e' makes it new) Mistick Village which is really a shopping center;

—Mystic Seaport, actually in Greenmanville, where saltwater history is elegantly displayed;

—Mystic, the gen-yew-ine article, where the bridge is raised and often lowered (if it doesn't stick) once each summertime hour to a chorus of local groans. To add to mystical jollity, the Stonington side of the bridge was formerly called Mystic Bridge, and the Groton side formerly was called Mystic River... which formerly formerly was known as Portersville, not to be confused with Porter's Rocks just up the river aways. Nobody seems to know who Porter was, which is probably just as well;

—West Mystic which has lots of houses and a post office but no grocery store.

(All of these Mystics took some getting used to. About two years for the publisher.)

But wait. There's Noank too, blessedly untainted by the 'Mystic' handle. Noank's a fine little village at the mouth of the river on the west side.

And there's Mason Island on the eastern side of the river. It's most often and erroneously called Mason's Island. Occasionally it appears as Masons Island. Future cartographers may bend to common usage... or add two more islands to the landscape.

Add Mouse Island and Ram Island - not too long ago known as, of course, Mystic Island - and most of the above places (forget Swantown and the City of Groton, forget indeed) delineate the confines of this collection.

We discovered that along the river is a nice place to live. Its heritage is more or less protected, if not in law then in consensus. Pride of place and a willingness to work for that intangible are dominant forces. They will assure that in another hundred years the area will not be totally condominiumized.

This is one of the most phytogenic places you'll ever see, for it is abundantly treed, shrubbed, lawned, and flowered. Probably more trees have been planted and nurtured here in the last ten years than were cut (or blown) down in a century. May and October are usually glorious.

An anthology is a free-spirited kind of thing to publish, for neither editor nor publisher has to take blame for any inaccuracies, only for selection of what shall be included or excluded and the way the ingredients are cut down to fit a given format.

Certainly every effort was made for this Anthology to be accurate and forthright, to correct grammar and punctuation where mistakes were too obvious or cumbersome, but to retain an essence while trimming the fat.

This anthology was fun to put together. And we learned a lot in distilling 300-plus years and ten generations into some 180 pages. Possibly some sacred cows were bullied along the way (Mason vs. Mason's or Masons), but no meanness was intended. And even in decorous Mystic — Bridge or River or Old or West — we found great humor (the Civil War monument unveiling; and the revelation to a longtime resident of the existence of a trolley car smack dab in the middle of town). There were and are other laughs, not all of them engaged in by the summertime population of laughing gulls. Our risibilities are kindly ones.

As the editor explained, it's not, strictly speaking, a history. It's more of an overview intended primarily for Mystic's casual visitors who, curious, find something very appealing about the place. In 1987 there were something over 750 thousand visitors.

This book was designed for a readership which, we think, does not wish to be burdened by ponderous detail. Therefore it's made up of short "takes" which, in the aggregate appear to accomplish our purpose. There are a lot of these little things "..." which indicate something left out in the necessary shortening process.

Only a very few photographs are over two years old because it's really a book of currency. Photos are rarely cutlined, for they have been so placed in the text or on their own that descriptions are redundant or unnecessary.

Lastly, those distractions called footnotes and credit lines have been simplified to boxed numbers (text sources) and letters (photographs). Lists for each are published in front of the book under "Acknowledgements."

Peter C. Crolius

Appreciation

Thanks are due to a great many people from both this community and elsewhere. Helpers will know the level of their assistance and will, please, award themselves accordingly from a large reservoir of gratitude. Until publication there were no detractors.

WELCOME
TO
HISTORIC
MYSTIC
SETTLED 1654

The Land

The Valley

1a

The first name by which white men knew the river was Siccanemos, or River of the Sachem. De Laet, a Dutch geographer, drew it on a map of the area in 1616 for Captain Adrian Block, a Dutch explorer who sailed the New England coast in the early seventeenth century.

Barely five miles in length, the river really was an arm of the sea. It was navigable for about two miles from its mouth by vessels drawing as much as sixteen feet of water. Two miles upriver from Fishers Island Sound there was a bar of hard sand about fifteen rods in width that allowed only thirteen feet draft at high water. Above the bar the channel continued a sixteen foot depth nearly to the head of the river. The entire channel was crooked and required alert attention of the part of friend or foe, native or immigrant.

In the century of the area's settlement most people traveled by foot or by canoe or small sailing vessel. One who arrived by water passed several small islands covered by scrubby growth. These came to be called Mouse, Penny, Sixpenny, Mason's, Abigail, Andrews, and Dodge Islands. Sixpenny Island was wooded and valuable enough to become a property grant in itself.

The largest island at the mouth of the river later belonged to one John Mason and his name was given to it.

Proceeding upriver beyond the sheltered harbor, the newly-arrived white man observed high, rocky cliffs at intervals on both sides. Heavy woods of white oak, ash, cedar, pine and spruce were nearby. The meandering channel with its strong tides and currents, sunken rocks, and hidden mudbanks, claimed his attention, but so did the numbers of points of land extending into the river. Some were wooded and some were covered with marsh grasses which looked like good prospective hay for cattle. These promontories were to become ideal sites for building and launching vessels, but the early settlers first looked for farm and pasture lands.

On the west bank and running approximately parallel with it was a high steep ridge for about half the length of the river. A brook joined the river from the west, then the land rose again steeply in a transverse, rolling ridge, one of several at the base of a highland that was observable far at sea which came to be known as Lantern Hill. At the head of the river, another stream, powerful little Mystic, or Mystick Brook poured in its deposits of silt carried from the highlands to the north. Here lay some good farm land.

At the beginning of colonization in 1650 the settlers did not select landholdings around a common. Most immigrants came by water and many chose parcels of land "laid out a hundred poles in breadth" along the river which brought them to their settling place. Theirs were scattered holdings and each was removed from any neighbor's claim for a number of years. As late as the Revolution less than two dozen houses dotted the length of the Mystic River.

2 History: Senegal and Beer Bottles

After the mountain building and metamorphic event of North America's collision with Europe, about 370 mya, this region was intruded by a massive dark magma approximately 18 square miles in area. Since the magma was very viscous it did not extrude through fissures to the surface, several miles above. Instead, it pushed up and domed the overlying rock to form a laccolith.

The intrusion was so massive that cooling progressed very slowly forming a coarse grained basalt called a gabbro.

. . .

Thrust faulting occurred in this region (probably when we hit Africa 250 mya) producing the S.E. moving wedge of Putnam gneiss which created the Honey Hill and Lake Char faults. This coincides with the time of the great Appalachian orogeny. When the collision between Africa and North America created the Appalachians and the whole east coast of North America was given to us, it was a gift from Senegal, West Africa.

. . .

The hydrothermal soaking by the granite fluids probably occurred during the time of the continental collision. Lantern Hill silica may have formed at this time.

. . .

Lantern Hill can be thought of as a silica (or quartz) dike that came up into the existing gneiss and later became exposed by differential erosion. Some interpret Lantern Hill as a completely replaced granite mass which has been converted into quartz by an alteration of the minerals of the granite and by the addition of silica from quartz-bearing solutions entering the rock.

Long Pond on the west side of the hill looks like a glacial fiord. It is easy to picture the ice caps moving south overhead, bulldozing rock debris at the frontal zone and finally coming to rest just south of here, forming a terminal moraine which we call Long Island and Fishers Island.

. . .

Park on a clearing to hike up the trail to the top of Lantern Hill. This 15-minute medium grade hike will reward you with a complete view of southeastern Connecticut. You will be immediately impressed with the rounded slopes of all of the surrounding hills. Not long ago a glacier moved south over this area and pushed over all of the pinnacles and irregularities normally found in an unglaciated region. Domal hills of morainal waste called drumlins are scattered about. A large drumlin called Bailey Hill is found just south of the Submarine Base in Groton.

To the south of the hill, Ottawa Silica Company can be seen tearing down another spectacular white silica formation. This silica is pulverized and much of it goes to Knox Glass Company in Dayville to make beer bottles. The quarry is not accessible to the public but had yielded find quartz crystal specimens to earlier collectors.

(The sun shining on the white quartz crystals created a 'lantern' to guide sailors coming into port. A watch was maintained here during the war of 1812.)

3

More Real Estate

As you look out across Fisher's Island sound it is interesting to consider that 10,000 years ago, when much of the ocean's water was contained in the glaciers that covered New England, the sea level was about 200 feet lower. Long Island Sound and part of the Continental Shelf was dry land. Indians living here at that time settled and fished along a coastline 50 miles further out.

When the glaciers melted they dropped all of the rocks and dirt that had caught in the ice when it was pushing south. Fisher's Island is really a pile of rubble left by the last retreating glacier!

2

Kettleholes

Most kettleholes in New England are still in the water table and have developed into bogs. Ledyard's kettleholes are dry and therefore present a unique educational opportunity to learn about glacial history.

Kettleholes are depressions formed by ice blocks that broke off or were left by the receding glacier. These ice blocks were covered by sand, in the outwash plain of a melting glacier, and later when the blocks melted the sand slumped into the place they had occupied forming the depression called a kettlehole.

Every effort should be made to preserve this area, with its classic surficial geology, from rapidly encroaching development which now threatens it. It has been proposed that a glacial park be established by Ledyard to preserve this valuable natural resource.

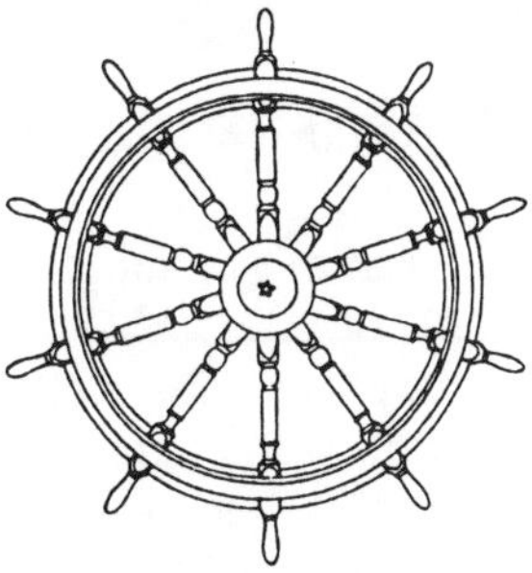

Portersville 1847

4

I ought to sing our noble river
On whose banks yon colors quiver.
It rises up in Lantern Hill
Driving many a cotton mill,
It sweeps right through River-Head
Nor stops at Long Bar's sandy bed,
But passing swiftly Helme's bridge,
Randall's wharf, the fort's high ridge
In whirling eddies round the bend
Near Murphy's point, which is lands end,
By Crow Point's dreary shore,
Leaving Fitches Goat Point store,
By Sixpence Isle, and Penny too,
Of Noank we've the finest view;

. . .

So there you have the river Mystic,
In all its glory, grand, majestic.
With Mallory's wharves and Cottrill's yard
Nor must we Randalls disregard
Nor Fishes' wharf, nor Mr. Avery's
Nor Iron's ways,
Nor Prentice's slip,
Nor Niles place where Baptists dip.
Here's Pequot hill, where they battled,
Where bows were bent and bullets rattled.
Here live the names long found in story
The Denisons, in all their glory.
The Burrowses of every race,
The Packers too have spread apace;
Parkses, Wolf, Gallup, Lamb,
Eldredge, Douglass and Brayman;
Fishes, Randalls, Averys, Tifts,
Haleys, Starks, Williams, Clifts.
These had their day and have it yet,
But new comers line each street.
Every year these new ones come
(Some had better staid at home).
But never mind, the world is free,
There's room enough for you and me.

1b Wooden Ships and Iron Men

Even before the puritan migration, England was experiencing a shortage of suitable timber. Since many of the pioneers came from maritime districts, they knew the value of good oak and stout, pine spars. A sound proportion of them were skilled ship's carpenters.

To utilize ship timber, two things were necessary - gently sloping banks of deep, sheltered channels, where ships could be laid down and launched safely, and broad, tidal rivers stretching inland to tap the forests which alone could supply the raw materials.

New England had a thousand coves and tidal streams. Some offered a dozen natural shipyard sites; others but one or two. All provided safe launching places and the material at one's elbow for scores of staunch plantation-built craft - huge, fine grained white oak, thick cedars, lofty white pine and spruce and tall white ash. The ideal

timber was there for the taking - both for building the ships and freighting them with spars, plank, boat boards, shingles, clapboards and staves.

. . .

Probably no port was more favorably designed by nature for the industry than the present New London County... Every mile or two along the entire coast of New London County, tidal streams thrust deeply northward into magnificent stands of hardwood. Each channel afforded ready made yards and tapped vast timber resources. One of these, to which the Indians had given the name "Mistick" was barely five miles in length. Yet a little village was to be established on its shores which was to become famous wherever ships floated, and which, for a time, *was to produce more noted captains, a greater tonnage of fine ships and a larger number of important sailing records than any place of its size in the world.*

. . .

Charles Mallory's first appearance in the present village of Mystic: He had just finished his apprenticeship to a sailmaker in New London and had started to walk to Boston, where he hoped to find employment. He crossed early Christmas morning, 1816, from New London to Groton on the ferry. It was unseasonably warm, so he took off his shoes, slinging them over his shoulder with his little pack of sailmaker's tools and proceeded on his way, barefoot. Coming down the hill into Mystic, he saw some boys playing ball in the fields where the present village stands, and joined them, boy fashion. However, he did not fail to note that there was quite a fleet of vessels moored nearby, and decided to stop over a few days on the chance of securing work. His first month's labor netted him thirty dollars. Within a few years he was accounted one of Mystic's leading citizens and in 1860, or thereabouts, he was one of the wealthiest shipowners of Connecticut.

At the time of young Mallory's arrival, Mystic shipping consisted principally, if not entirely, of small coasting and fishing vessels. Some of this, if family tradition is accepted, made winter voyages to the West Indies and occasional trips across the Atlantic, but long voyages and especially foreign voyages were still the exception. This was shortly to be changed.

Two new factors contributed to shape Mystic's destiny on the sea:

[1] Southern fishing and salvage operations proved very remunerative and supplied Mystic citizens with the means for entering into direct trade with the South. Boys from the home town began to settle in Southern ports, as representatives of Mystic shipowners or to engage in trade on their own account. Within a few years they were scattered from Baltimore to Texas. Two of them founded Key West in 1819. Others established

---

To come to an anchor with the wind aft.

First, hand the main topsail, and then lower the fore topsail down on the cap; and when you are within a reasonable distance of the place where you mean to drop anchor, (which distance is to be judged of from the readiness of the ship to obey the helm, and from her velocity) the tiller may be put either one way or the other, the fore topsail and fore topmast staysail clued up and taken in, the mizen topsail braced sharp up, and the mizen sheet hauled flat aft. When the ship ranges close to the wind, she is, as it were, lying to under the mizen and mizen top sails, with the last mentioned sail full or a-back according as you may have occasion to shoot a-head or drop a-stern; so that if you are too much to windward of the spot where you mean to bring to, you drift till you arrive at it: if you are precisely in the proper birth, you let go the anchor in lowering down the mizen topsail, which is to be furled as soon as the vessel is brought up; then the ship will come head to wind by the power of the mizen which must be brailed up as soon as it shakes.

prosperous industries in Georgia and Louisiana.

[2] The second factor in the development of Mystic was the sealing industry. Mystic men and vessels first engaged in this new enterprise under the leadership of Edmund Fanning in 1819.

. . .

It was a hard, dangerous business, but it provided Mystic men with the means to build more ships and engage in new ventures. In particular, it enabled them to enter the whaling industry, which was destined to become the principal activity of the seaport from 1830 to 1850, or thereabouts.

Whaling, however, got off to a slower start than sealing. For one thing it was more expensive. A whole fleet of sealers could be outfitted for the cost of a whaleship of average size, together with its outfit for a long voyage. The business also required a much longer apprenticeship to acquire the indispensable skill, as well as a knowledge of whaling grounds and the habits of whales.

. . .

From first to last, Mystic had twenty-seven large whaleships and barks, averaging well over 300 tons register, besides a number of brigs and schooners used principally as tenders in the sea elephant hunting. As this was during a period when her population never exceeded 1,500, it is obvious that Mystic must have been a very busy community. The peak came in 1845, and the business thereafter slowly declined, and shortly after the outbreak of the Civil War, her last whaler was sold.

. . .

In 1853 the principal locations of Mystic shipbuilding were fixed, for ninety years to come. Aside from the Palmer firm, near the mouth of the river, most of the

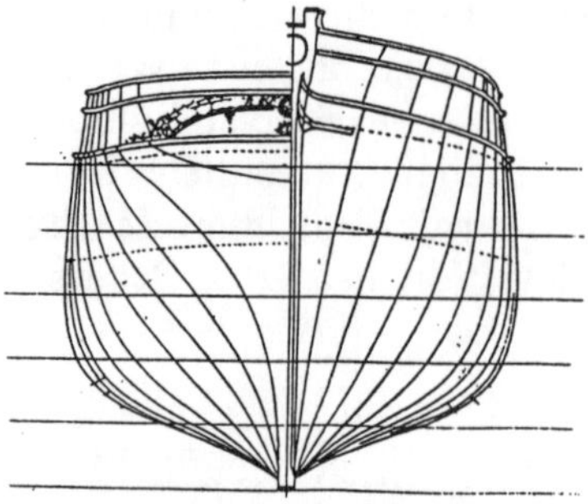

important work of Mystic proper was to be done in four yards - the Mallory and Greenman yards, the Irons & Grinnell yard (later Hill & Grinnell and still later Pendleton Brothers) and Maxson & Fish (later the Alexander Irving yard).

. . .

Shipbuilding on the Mystic has spanned the greater part of three centuries. Its greatest activity falls into two decades from 1850 to 1870. During this period the little village produced a greater tonnage of fine ships and steamers than any other place of equal size in America, if not in the world. Altogether, twenty-two vessels rated as clippers were built here in addition to a large number of passenger packets, brigs, schooners and ships. During the four years of the Civil War, fifty-six steamships were constructed in the three yards then operating, many of them ranging up to 230 feet and more in length, the largest measuring 250 feet. Even the boilers and machinery were for the most part built and installed here.

After the close of the Civil War, Mystic continued to build ships and steamers in considerable numbers for another five years. During this time, also the four principal yards launched some of the finest "Cape Horners" of the period - several of them large three deckers.

. . .

However, the demand for wooden sailing vessels was falling off. The lessons of the Civil War had bred a new respect for iron steamers. Much of the new wooden construction was going to Maine as Mystic timber was exhausted and the resultant increased cost gave "Down East" yards a steadily growing advantage. The competition of Pacific Coast builders was also increasing.

The last full rigged Mystic ships were launched in 1869 - the *Frolic* by Greenman and the *Dauntless* by Maxson & Fish. Thereafter, local construction was restricted in the main to schooners, lighters, barges and steamers, with a growing emphasis on fast sailing small craft - yachts, pilot boats and fishermen.

One cannot even venture a guess as to the number of vessels built on the Mystic during the century and a quarter which elapsed between the launching of the first ship in 1662 and 1789, the year the United States customs Service was established. The number was undoubtedly substantial, but, for the most part, even the names have been lost.

It has been possible, however, to determine definitely that 869 vessels have been built here since 1789. The list included sloops of 30 tons and upwards, schooners up to 2,000 tons, clipper ships and packets of 1,700 tons and steamships of 3,500 tons and more. It includes 22 clipper ships, 118 steamers, and 20 yachts.

This aggregate is by no means complete. It does not contain any of the numerous larger yachts and fishing vessels built during the past 40 years. It omits all sloops and schooners and other vessels built during a period of about fifty years. These and many more vessels are excluded because no precise information is available other than that they were built in the townships of Stonington or Groton. Still others are missing, owing to gaps in the custom house records. All things considered, it is reasonable to assume that a complete tally for the past 156 years would exceed 1,000 vessels by a substantial margin.

. . .

Mystic developed every trade represented in building and outfitting ships. It had ropewalks, sail and rigging lofts, ship chandlers, cooper shops, block and trunnell makers, spar yards, figurehead carvers' shops, mast hoop makers, shipsmith shops, and even a hardy specialist who made wedges and barrel bungs.

. . .

The men of mystic were for the most part descendants of those who left England to gain freedom, both material and spiritual. Their ancestors, by chance, had settled on a coast where the conditions of life were as harsh and difficult as any encountered by early colonists. It was a land of rocks, swamps, pathless forests and sterile soil. It could be protected and made habitable only by efforts which called for the utmost in determination and endurance.

Moreover, the district was so situated that for two centuries its people were exposed by land and sea to every danger that threatened. It was the thin, cutting edge of America - its inhabitants were expendable. Indians first, then French, Spanish and British harried its people. Through the seventeenth and eighteenth centuries the war alert never ceased its clamor. From 1775 to 1815 there was hardly a moment of respite from threat of capture, or loss of life and property.

Year after year the people of Mystic survived on land or won safety at sea only by exercise of the most arduous efforts and the utmost skill and courage. They and communities situated like them, constituted America's thin, outer-line of defense. Many another noted spot had its day of trial. Mystic had its thousand days.

Whortleberries and Bones

44

From early settlers we learn that the hills around the river and parts of Masons Island were burned over each year to encourage the growth of huckleberries, first called whortleberries and then hurtleberries. A part of the "Great Plain" was burned over two years ago, killing the trees and brush. It is now thick with huckleberry bushes. Dried berries were a staple of the Indian diet. After the Mason family settled on the Island, their sheep and cattle continued to keep down the brush and trees. There are probably many more trees on Masons Island today than there have been for several hundred years.

The Indians left few traces on the Island. Some arrowheads and a stone ax have been found. At the north end of the present pond was a spring which still feeds it. Before the road was built there, I uncovered a sizable shell heap and found a black wampum bead and the bowl fragment of an English clay pipe. Mrs. Minnie Wilson Lorello, one-time resident of the Island, recalls an Indian burying ground south of Wolf Ledge, as well as one at the south end of Coconke Point on the mainland. A grave was excavated there in 1912, but nothing was found but bones.

H

Weather

5a

Mail and Military Weather

A frame hung up in the Mystic River post office gives notice that, by an arrangement between the War and Post Office Departments, daily bulletins concerning the probabilities of the weather are to be sent to post offices which can be conveniently reached by such dispatches from regular signal stations. Thus, farmers, fishermen and others, whose business depends upon the weather, are to have the benefit of the careful observations of the

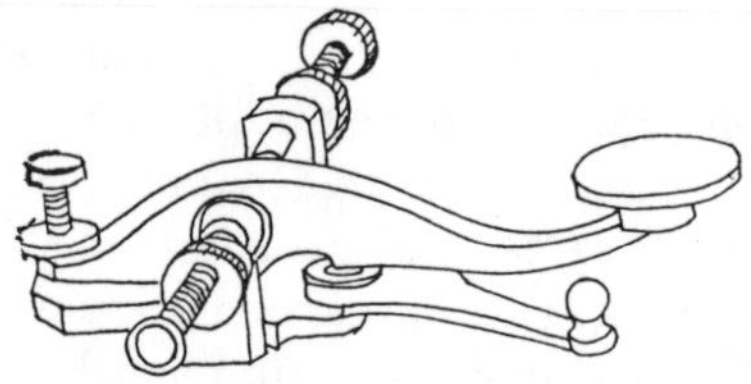

signal corps throughout the country, and of the abstruse calculations and suggestions therefrom by their head at Washington, to take the place of "Daboll's" prophecies, and guesses by the moon. These "probabilities" are becoming more and more reliable, and will be a great help to the classes mentioned, in forecasting and laying out their work.

6

The Blizzard of '88

On Monday, March 12, 1888, a tremendous blizzard struck the eastern seaboard of the United States, causing havoc from Maryland to Maine. Early in the storm, all seventy-four telegraph wires between Washington and Baltimore blew down, and by the end of Monday almost every other wire in the East was down too.

. . .

Hundreds of trains were stalled for days, immobilized by twenty- and thirty-foot snow drifts. In the cities public transportation ceased, businessmen could do no business, coal supplies dwindled, and babies were crying for milk. At sea the storm was a hurricane, with winds up to ninety miles an hour. Waves three stories high pounded on the rocks of New England and crashed across the beaches of Long Island, New Jersey, and Delaware. One hundred and ninety-eight ships were either sunk, damaged, or driven ashore, and nearly a hundred seamen died. On land the death toll came to more than three hundred, by accident, freezing, or storm-caused illness.

To rank as a true blizzard a storm must combine heavy snowfall, bitter cold, and a fierce wind that mingles the snow in the air with the snow on the ground, whirling it madly about until anyone in its midst can see almost nothing else. Such snow is not soft and pretty,

but consists of tiny, sharp particles of flying ice that sting and cut. And all this continues without much surcease for two to three days.

. . .

In smaller places and in the country, people were still living a simpler life and had time-honored ways of dealing with storms. They stayed home and turned to supplies laid in during the previous autumn; they didn't miss electricity, or running water, or telephones because they weren't used to them; nor did they look to anyone but themselves and their neighbors to plow the roads. If no help appeared for days, they could wait.

. . .

Amen to that, Professor

6

Professor Cleveland Abbe, founder and organizer of the United States Weather Service, was the person best qualified to analyze the blizzard, now that it was over, and to explain what had been going on up there and why it had all been so inadequately predicted.

"The element that fooled us was the ocean winds, about which we never had any warning," he said. "You see, we know so little anyway, and there is so much more of which we are and must be ignorant..."

5b

Snowbound

It will be no news to the readers of the Press in the Eastern States that the snowstorm of Monday and Tuesday was in many respects the worst of the season and in some respects the worst in this region for many years.

In Mystic and vicinity on Tuesday morning and forenoon it was rainy and windy and not cold enough to snow, and people were inclined to treat the story that a snowstorm caused the failure of trains and mails from New York as a canard, but when no mail arrived from west of New London during the day and in the afternoon, the wind increased to a gale, and towards night snow began to fall, seeing was believing and from five to eight o'clock a veritable blizzard, such as but few of the young people had ever seen or experienced, prevailed. It was with the utmost difficulty that men could get from their places of business to their homes and few returned for the evening. The wind, which had been northeasterly during the day, was now from the northwest, and the air was literally full of snow, so that a strong man could face it but a short time, and without any guide or landmark like a fence or a row of buildings he would inevitably be lost in a very few minutes. Mr. L. A. Morgan of the grocery, who has a severe cold, undertook to go to his home in a hack, but when they arrived at the top of Pros-

pect Hill Mr. Clift could not make the horses face the wind to go north-ward, so he was obliged to leave his passenger to spend the night at the hospitable mansion of Captain R.P. Wilbur, within 40 rods of his own home. Others had pretty sharp experiences, but up to the present writing, no casualties are reported near by.

The storm continued with unabated force Tuesday night and our older citizens say that it was not surpassed "since the year and day John Minturn was lost," February 15th, 1845.

Forecasting

7

"With the rain before the wind,
Your topsail halliards you must mind;
But when the wind's before the rain,
You may hoist your topsails up again."

"First rise, after very low,
Indicates a stronger blow."

"When the sun sets in a clear,
An easterly wind you need not fear."

Head in the Clouds

7

Soft-looking or delicate clouds, foretell fine weather, with moderate or light breezes; hard edged, oily-looking clouds, wind. A dark gloomy blue sky is windy; but a light, bright blue sky indicates fine weather. Generally, the *softer* the clouds look, the less wind (but perhaps more rain) may be expected; and the harder, more 'greasy,' rolled, tufted, or ragged, the stronger the coming wind will prove. Also a bright yellow sky at sunset presages wind; a pale yellow, wet; and thus, by the prevalence of red, yellow, or gray tints, the coming weather may be foretold very nearly; indeed, if aided by instruments, almost exactly.

Small inky-clouds foretell rain; a light scud, driving across heavy clouds, wind and rain; but if alone, wind only.

High upper clouds crossing the sun, moon, or stars, in a direction different from that of the lower clouds or wind then blowing, foretell a change of wind (beyond tropical latitudes).

After fine, clear weather, the first signs (in the sky) of change, are usually small, curly, streaked, or spotty clouds, followed by an overcasting of vapor that grows into cloudiness. This murky appearance, more or less oily or watery, as wind or rain will prevail, is a sure sign. The higher and more distant the clouds seem to be, the more gradual, but extensive, the coming change of weather will prove.

Generally speaking, natural, quiet, delicate tints or colors, with soft, undefined forms of clouds, foretell fine weather; but gaudy, or unusual hues, with hard, definite outlines, presage rain and wind.

7

Hurricanes

June, too soon;
July, stand by;
August, look out you must;
September, remember;
October, all over.

8a

1815

Sept. 23-24 - The Great Hurricane - many ships driven ashore; 4 of 10 houses at Mystic Bridge destroyed; in Borough debris 15 ft. high on Water St., and much land washed away from the sides of the Point; bridge over Lambert's Cove, built by lottery 50 yrs. before, destroyed. At the Point wife and infant child of Capt. Benj. Morrill with Mrs. Haven, a relative, and Miss Mott of Block Island swept to sea in their home and drowned. Only other Borough house totally destroyed was that of Widow Anna Loper whose 16-yr.-old son, Richard F. Loper, carried her to safety.

9

Just You Wait

If, as a Southern New Englander, you were born before 1929, chances are you reckon all the world's history as being either *before* or *after September 21st, 1938.* No matter what violence of wind and water hits these shores in the future - and it's a dead certainty it will - it'll be contrasted (only similar things can be compared and nothing will ever be similar) to the '38 Hurricane... and be belittled by it. Physical evidence of the cataclysm can still be seen here and there today, some 47 years after that destructive afternoon, and awe and fear from it is well fixed in older minds and tongues.

Mystic Snippets

10f

The wind began to blow. It eased a dozen shingles from the roof of the West Mystic post office and railroad station. Robert D. Bradley went after them, picked them up, and carried them inside. Another gust tore off another dozen. Mr. Bradley continued his retrieving. He gave it up when the shingles began flying off in lots of a hundred - and carried his building to a spot where it blocked the road.

An electric refrigerator from a Lindbergh Road house was carried a half mile by wind and water to a point across the Post Road, then stolen.

A West Mystic man who owned cows and a barn took the animals into his home when the barn blew

down.There is no sense talking about damage done to buildings and trees. It can be seen wherever one looks. When a wind snaps 12 by 12 timbers, it's a wind.

Horns on automobiles in the lowlands became "shorted" by the water and blew until the batteries wore out. Railroad crossing lights tolled an unnecessary warning during the night.

Only three pleasure craft still in the water in Mystic were insured for the storm. They were the only ones to escape serious damage.

A local real estate agent was about to consummate a building sale when the property was blown down.

1938: "A mite airy, ain't it, Francis?"

11

As the hurricane belted its way north, those in its path continued to be generally unaware of what was coming, because it imposed upon areas already devastated a tragically effective pattern of isolation.

Communications, by land, sea, phone, telegraph, or teletype, were mostly wiped out in those areas which had most to communicate; the system fell apart piecemeal, and even where electric power or telephones still functioned, the information coming out of places battered by the storm was fragmentary and confused. In communities worst hit, even if anyone had been able to piece together what had happened, the transmission of news was low on the priority list of what needed to be done.

Looking back, I think principally it is as well in instances of massive disaster that one does not know everything at once. There are limits to what the human creature can comprehend and bear in a hurry. I suppose it was as well that we did not know then what had befallen Long Island. Nor did we know that Connecticut was next.

On Saturday, September 24, three days after the hurricane, the New York *Herald Tribune* reported on page 1 that author Elmer Davis was missing from Mason Island, off Mystic, Connecticut. Actually, he wasn't; he did, however, share with thousands the extraordinary experience of being forced to accept the reality of the hurricane.

"When the wind began to blow about 2 o'clock Wednesday afternoon, most of the inhabitants of these parts were convinced that it was only the traditional 'line storm,' the three-day blow that comes every September when the sun crosses the equator," Davis said. "Even as the wind rose and its tone changed to the ee-ee-ee that well-read persons recognize as the mark of the hurricane, even when the rain came in horizontal sheets, and tightly closed windows began to leak streams of water, traditionalists insisted that this couldn't be a hurricane because there never had been a hurricane in these latitudes...

"And then all at once in a thousand households, the argument stopped and everybody began to nail up all the doors and windows and hope that with all the air shut out, the wind would not take the whole house along in one piece. With every window, every door fastened as tightly shut as you could get it, you sat in the living room and watched the shingles on the garage roof ruffle up like a hen's feathers blown in the wind and then, one by one, tear off and whirl away. You saw nearby trees slowly lean over and go down; you listened to the crash of breaking windows; the steady ee-ee-ee of the wind, you felt the floor waving under you like a shaken carpet."

When the sea rose 14 feet above normal at Mason Island, Carolyn Wilson, a former Chicago correspondent, looked up, while trying to plug leaks in her wall, to find the ocean at her door when it ought to have been one hundred yards away. She had to get out and tried to take her cat with her, but he refused to go, so she kissed him a dolorous good-bye and swam a half-mile over drowned shrubbery to high ground.

. . .

Mrs. Orris B. Norman was in Old Mystic... "I had just started my afternoon stint in the Old Mystic post office, where I was also postmaster, janitor, and clerk, and when the window blinds began to bang, I tried to steady my jittery nerves by reading a magazine article.

"I reckoned the stone building, more than a century old, with walls about two feet thick, was the safest place in an affair of this kind. But I soon changed my mind. Believe it or not, the building began to rock perceptibly and the desk began to jump. That's about the time I got hysterical and decided it was time to close up."

. . .

"The next morning, everywhere I went, I saw faces full of misery and despair, as people who had barely been hanging on and trying to get along the best they could surveyed incalculable damage to their properties. I heard many stories of a miserable night spent in roofless and sometimes wall-less houses or how they had taken refuge with neighbors in the night. I saw parents who had spent the night worrying about children who had not returned from school. I saw people worrying about relatives and friends they could not communicate with and about whose safety they feared. I saw barns flattened to the ground. Hardly a barn was left standing in

the whole village. Hen coops and other such light buildings never were found. The streets were strewn with broken elms and other trees, many of which I had to crawl over or under in order to get through. I went up and surveyed the ruins of the Baptist church."

. . .

And near Mystic, Mrs. James F. Stark, in attempting to fix a window of her home during the storm, was struck by a piece of flying glass that severed her jugular vein. She bled to death.

12 1944

Six years after the Great Hurricane of 1938 another storm hit the area. The New London Day of September 13, 1944 reported that a hurricane would hit this area that night. They were right and at 8:45 P.M. the next evening the storm hit with its full fury. This time the public had been warned in time to take precautions. Schools were dismissed at noon and people moved from low lying areas to higher ground. Windows were boarded up and family possessions were moved to upper floors or to safer locations. The winds blew at 70 MPH with gusts to 95 MPH. Trees were uprooted and power and telephone lines went down. The next day the newspapers reported that two people had died but property damage was not as great as the 1938 hurricane because the public was warned and prepared.

12 Carol

For the third time in 16 years another hurricane struck this area. September 1, 1954 Hurricane Carol came ashore. At the shipyard and Willow Point the storm wreaked havoc. Four or five sleek yachts were sunk and many wrecked on shore. Launching and storage cradles went up the river with the tide. The managers of the shipyard figured their loss was $25,000 according to the new London *Day*. Main streets of Mystic were under four feet of water. A young couple, Mr. and Mrs. Link, camping on Mystic Island were trapped when their boat was swept away in the storm. They crouched in an old foundation for safety and were rescued in the evening.

The Right Stuff

Conviction

10a

On the morning of the fourth of July the committee who had charge of the Liberty Pole, so called, attempted to raise the United States flag on the same. In this they were violently opposed by Capt. Thomas Williams the owner of the land upon which the pole stands. Capt. W. denied the right of the committee to raise a flag upon the pole, and though a very aged man, he stoutly maintained his demand. A large and angry crowd gathered on the spot, in which the sympathy was entirely on one side. Hot and angry words were passed when Capt. Williams, to carry his point, with palsied and quivering limbs climbed to the crosstrees, a distance of more than sixty feet and cut the halyards...

Bingeing

13

Not many days ago, one of our citizens (a grocer and dealer in various kinds of articles to replenish the inner man) was entertaining a number of friends, at his store in Mystic River, when, by his superior conversational powers, or the use of some other means equally as potent, they all began to wax exceedingly merry; not to say gloriously happy and boisterous - so much so, indeed, that on going into his house on some errand our worthy host gave unmistakable evidence to his better half that he was not, as he termed it, "exactly - hic - apropos" - so taking advantage of his good nature and accommodating disposition, she contrived to persuade him to remain there a short time, while she attended to the store. This feat of diplomacy accomplished, she took the broom and repaired to the scene of merry-making, and after setting open the front door in a very inviting manner, a few flourishes and evolutions of that potent sceptre of female

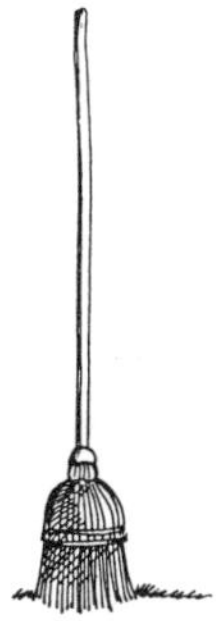

power conveyed to the minds of the astonished occupants, in language more eloquent than words, the fact that their presence was no longer needed in that particular locality, and they were not slow to profit by such unmistakable suggestions.

Soon after, the aforesaid citizen was arrested on complaint of Alexander Gray, and brought before the proper legal tribunal to answer to the charge of violating the statutes of the sovereign State of Connecticut, by selling, causing to be sold or giving away intoxicating drinks, and fined twenty dollars with costs. The money not being forthcoming, the body of the prisoner was conveyed to appropriate lodgings in New London. But after twenty-four hours, spent, no doubt, in serious reflection and meditation, our hero concluded to shell out the required tin and brush off the dust of his feet against a hotel which had nothing to recommend it to public patronage but the fact that board and lodgings were furnished gratis.

5h

Duty

Our attention has been called to the statement, published in some of the papers without explanation, or with unfavorable comment that while his sons lay dead or dying at his home, Mr. Langworthy went his usual round with milk on Monday morning. We have been assured that Mr. L. who had been up all night, and could not and would not rest, was urged by a gentleman who was there, and by other friends, to go his usual route, as a means of getting his mind - which was evidently suffering from the strain - off from the distressing circumstances at his home, and as he is a man who does not stop to ask what people will say, when he chooses to do a thing, he went as advised.

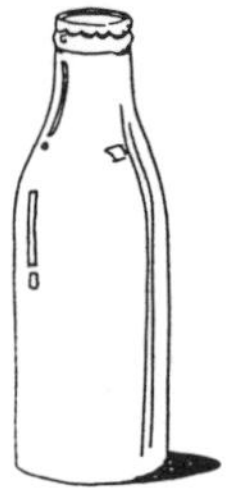

8b

The Grand Old Man of Whitehall

In his young, palmy, halcyon days, admired, feted, and respected by all, Richard Stonebridge, Esquire, was the most promising young man of the town, and the "best match," for whose capture all the bright beauties of the valley "set their caps." Straight as an Apollo, with a style like "Brummel," and an imperial air, he seemed worthy of earth's loveliest and best, and his courage and bravery shown upon several occasions made him the admiration of the noblest hearts of the country. His father died when Richard was at a tender age, and left him the

possessor of a noble farm, "Whitehall," to which his own talents and industry had added two more landed estates in other parts of the same town.

. . .

Within the memory of many now residing in Mystic Valley, an old man, bent under the weight of years, but with an eye bright and piercing as an eagle's, clothed in garments of so many colors that the original was difficult to distinguish, his nose and chin such near neighbors that aught but friendship between them would have been impossible, wearing the meanest of brogans, and a most shocking hat covered with grease and filth, from under which a few scattered locks of white hair escaped, wandering restlessly about the streets of the village, living upon crusts of the refuse of the tables of the benevolent, but still in his own right the possessor of thousands, both in real estate and stocks.

. . .

The contrast was so great, so terrible and disgusting, between this man who won all hearts, and whose form was the perfection of manly beauty, and the miserable, wretched, starved and half-clad miser who went by the familiar sobriquet of "Uncle Dick," as almost to exceed belief.

His personal appearance, in his parched and tattered dress, bent nearly double with age and infirmities, was so pitiful as to excite sympathy, until you conversed with him; then your dislike for the sordid passions of his soul killed out the humane feelings of your heart, and left only contempt and disgust. He went about the streets, his piercing undimmed eye fixed upon the ground, as though his miserly soul sought some hidden wealth in the dust. To any noble heart, death would have been far preferable to the punishment this man received by being given over to the predominant passions of his own breast; but to his avaricious soul life had no other value, but as a lengthened opportunity to acquire and amass wealth for its own sake. He sought it, not to bestow on the poor, the unfortunate, the starving; for, during his long life of fourscore years, he was never known to give one penny to benevolence; neither desired he it for any purpose less worthy, but in itself commendable; but he craved it, he clutched for it, and grasped it with the longing feelings of the miser, and chuckled in his inmost soul at the addition of every farthing to his hoard. If punishment was terrible, and if it is eternal I can imagine none other so fearful.

. . .

He went about his farm as if in search of something he could never find, as though he sought a peace of mind which constantly evaded him. His eyes were bent upon the ground and they never met the full gaze of another; but instead of resorting to the cup to still the qualms of conscience, he gave way to his miserly habits, accumulating almost by instinct, never relaxing his grasp on a shilling or even a penny, literally throwing himself into the arms of his golden God, without any restrictions or reservations.

. . .

He lived to an extreme age, growing more and more in meanness, the scorn and contempt of his neighbors, and a byword in the mouths of all good men.

At length, as age crept upon him, he leased his farms, reserving in each house a room, where he saved, collected and treasured up all manner of worthless, broken articles, fragments of farming utensils, scraps of iron, pieces of crockery, bits of harness, old nails, and every imaginable thing he found in his travels, that he thought had, or might have a money value. In the year 1835 I was admitted into his reserved room in Whitehall, and the effect upon my boyish imagination will never be effaced; besides cart-loads of the articles enumerated... in one corner of the room was a quantity of "Continental money," which had, without doubt, drawn drops of blood from his infernal heart, because of its depreciation.

. . .

And in subsequent years, when I knew "Uncle Dick," and held long conversation with him, that room was ever present before me, and his life, a curse to himself and profitless to the world, led me to desire early death rather than an existence under so great excitement.

Plantation at Quoketaug

8k

In 1747, then, we have Nehemiah Williams II with his bride Abigail nicely situated in their new house at the end of the lane.

Nehemiah's house was nicely arranged and appointed. It contained seventeen rooms, most of them large, high ceilinged and very comfortable. The ell or rear portion of the house was devoted to service. Basically it was a very large kitchen surrounded by a small borning room, a sink room, cheese room, press room, and the dairy. Over these quarters was the garret which was primarily for storage.

The front part of the house consisted on the first floor of a large keeping room, a pantry, two large front chambers, and two small bedrooms and a large spin-

ning and weaving room that was rough and unfinished. It was here that wool was spun into yarn, flax into linen and the two were woven into fabric to adorn the beautifully appointed rooms.

. . .

Nehemiah II seems to have been a dapper man for his times and occupation. But as a planter he was probably the manager of his large estate. This does not mean that he did not work, but most of his time was probably spent in laying out and organizing the chores for his sons and slaves as well as indentured servants.

There were many slaves and at least one indentured servant on this farm. In fact in the north pasture of

the farm one can still see a depression in the ground that is supposedly the site of a cellar hole for a slaves' cabin. It is known that a family of slaves named Time worked on this farm, and that a black boy named Prince and a black girl named Lettuce provided much assistance in performing the daily chores of milking, haying, harvesting, hoeing and then making all the cheese and butter much of which was used for trade or barter. The female slaves probably assisted in the household chores helping Abigail to keep the seventeen rooms in order and to prepare the food for all of the family members and help. Much of the spinning and weaving was probably done by the ladies of the house, but the routine work no doubt was performed by the slaves.

Nehemiah's indentured servant was Amos Torns, a little Indian boy indentured to Nehemiah by his mother Sylva Torns. This agreement was made in 1789 and for it Nehemiah was to teach Amos to read the Bible and to feed and clothe him. In return Amos was to work on the farm. When Amos reached the age of twenty-one he was released and given two suits of clothes, one for "every-day and the other for hallows day." Perhaps there were other indentured servants on the place as well, but this indenture is the only one to survive the years and is in the possession of a descendent.

By the time the first national census was taken in 1790, there were several black citizens living in the area surrounding the Williams farm and possessing the same names that appeared in inventories of the family throughout the 18th century. These were probably former slaves who worked on the Williams farm.

To prevent cider-bottles from bursting.—When you bottle cider, place the bottles on the ground in the northerly part of the cellar, and cover them with moss, which you must keep constantly wet with cold water.

Moving

16

Prayer When The Bridge Is Up

O God of Life, Time, and Traffic, as I sit by the drawbridge, help me to keep cool. Let me not be pressured by schedules into rapping my fingers and gritting my teeth. And if I am tempted to tighten my grip on the wheel and curse under my breath, show me that I am only injuring myself and making no gains. Help me, Lord, to use this time of waiting constructively, calming myself. . . looking at this beautiful town with a relaxed eye. . . appreciating the people around me. . . and thanking you for this moment of silence. Let me be still. . . and know that thou art God. AMEN.

The Bridge

14a

In 1819 the Mystic Bridge Company contracted to build a bridge for $28,000. Toll was charged from 25 cents for a four-horse coach to 2 cents for a pedestrian. A drawbridge was needed to reach the shipyards up the river and in 1841 Col. Amos Clift rebuilt the bridge with a span which was lifted by a yoke of oxen. In 1865 Groton and Stonington voted to build a new bridge and a year later opened "the finest iron bridge in the state," 30 feet wide, equipped with a turntable to allow passage of vessels.

Trolleys clanged from Groton to Mystic in 1904 and service was extended to Stonington and Westerly the next year after the Mystic bridge was replaced by a structure able to bear the trolley's weight. The present bridge was built in 1921, financed by Groton, Stonington and the State. An unusual structure, its counterweights are above the bridge rather than below, where the water is too shallow. Few large ships sail up the Mystic nowadays, but in summertime the span is raised every hour to accommodate a stream of pleasure craft.

Britain - Booted Baptist Boatman Burrows

1a

Until 1660 there was no way to cross the river except by traveling around the head of the river or crossing in one's own boat. In 1660 the General Court of Connecticut appointed Robert Burrows as ferryman. He was empowered to charge a groat, four pence, to carry a man and a horse from his halfway house under the "mountain of rock" on the west bank to a point on the east bank halfway down the river's length. Thus the sparse settlements on each side of the river were linked and this was the beginning of the commercial transportation by water that was to figure so prominently in the area's later economic history.

(Burrows had come to New England with the Pilgrims. He had been driven out of Manchester, England, with his two brothers because they were Baptists.)

14b

The Trolleys

The Groton and Stonington Street Railway Company was chartered by the Connecticut legislature August 17, 1903, authorized to lay tracks from the Groton ferry landing through Poquonnock Bridge, Noank, Mystic and Stonington to the Rhode Island line at Westerly...The Groton-Mystic route opened to the public December 19th, 1904 and was completed the following year to the Rhode Island line...Known locally as "the G&S," this route was a single track line except for five turnouts where cars bound in opposite directions could pass. Power lines were strung between wooden poles 125 feet apart which also carried a telephone line for dispatching.

...

From the start the G&S was a profitable road, carrying 744,807 passengers the first six months.

...

The power source was at Mystic where electricity was generated on the river bank in a brick powerhouse with a 125-foot smokestack. Inside engines and generators hummed, their boilers heated by coal which barges

brought up the river directly to the station. Beside the powerhouse stood the carbarn with a capacity of eighteen cars.

In October 1904 the company's rolling stock was delivered — eight open cars for warm weather, four with thirteen wooden benches and four with fifteen; and eight closed cars each measuring forty feet overall, all purchased from the Jewett Car Company. The green closed

cars had green plush seats and five large double windows on each side with upper sashes of special Florentine glass.

In 1906 the G&S announced plans for a trolley freight service between Groton and Westerly, taking and discharging freight from local merchants at any white pole.

. . .

Express business was especially heavy in November 1910 after temperance forces lost an election in Stonington. Both the express car and work car were kept busy carrying consignments of wet goods for the Borough saloons...

In 1911 G&S laid additional track from Broadway, Mystic, three miles north to Old Mystic. This line opened September 21, 1911, but unfortunately never paid its way.

. . .

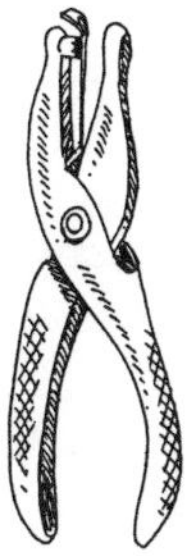

Labor troubles began in 1914. Employees threatened to strike, demanding an increase in pay and provision for motormen on open cars to be protected in stormy weather. They were granted a new pay scale — 22-1/2 cents per hour for beginning workers and up to 28-1/2 cents per hour for five year veterans.

. . .

In 1928 there was pressure to discontinue trolleys completely in favor of buses. On June 4, 1928 the Groton-Stonington Traction Company obtained permission to discontinue the unprofitable trolley service and substitute buses, and also were ordered to dismantle the line and take up the tracks.

. . . .

Some of the venerable trolleys which had carried so many workers and pleasure riders ended their days at Mystic. One car purchased there by Harry Bendett was converted into a lunch cart on Water Street. Others stood neglected on riverside property which was acquired in 1931 by the Mystic Art Association for their new gallery.

15a

Last of the Breed

When the G&S began business, its rolling stock included eight open cars, eight closed cars, a double-truck Taunton snowplow and a work car.

. . .

Harry Bendett lived on Water Street. About 1929 he bought two of the old trolleys. One, a passenger car, he located north of his house to use as a lunch wagon.

But Mystic still has a trolley. Besides the diner, Harry Bendett had acquired a second car, the old snowplow. He gave this to his son Henry. Today it stands a short distance east of Water Street near the Steamboat Wharf parking lot. Until his death a year ago, Henry used his old trolley for a radio shack. For more than fifty years he was an avid ham radio operator and had worked all states and worked all continents. The shack held his radio equipment.

Henry's friends called his old trolley a work car, but Henry told his sister emphatically during his last illness that it was the old Taunton snowplow. It doesn't look much like a trolley any more. The trucks disappeared long ago, and it squats close to the ground like an elongated shed.

Nevertheless, it is Mystic's last trolley, a relic of the days when street cars were the last word in travel.

17

Railroad Swing Bridge (1919)

Built by the American Bridge Co. in 1919, this is the only center-bearing swing-through truss on the former New York, New Haven and Hartford Railroad in Connecticut. There are four timber-trestle approach spans to the south (total length 46') and four similar approach spans to the north (46'). The swing span is a 181'-long rivet-connected Warren through truss with verticals.

The original operator's house, suspended over the tracks between the trusses, is now used for equipment storage and the bridge is controlled from an operator's house on the shore. Operating equipment has not been altered since initial installation. There is one 25-horsepower motor for operating the swing span and one for the rail locks, wedge locks and bridge locks. Timbers have been replaced occasionally in the approach spans and the swing span had some members replaced in 1946. This two-track bridge carries trains every day.
(*A new swing bridge was completed in 1981. Ed.*)

The Light on Morgan Point

18

Old Light List No.: 139 (Obsolete)
Location: Latitude 41° 18'57" N
Longitude 71° 59'03"W
Height: 52' (HAW 60')
Range: 12 miles
Lens: Sixth Order, 160 candlepower
Rebuilt: 1867-68
Discontinued: 1922

During the American Revolution and the War of 1812, there was neither spindle nor beacon to mark the mouth of the channel of the Mystic River. American frigates, clipper ships, schooners, and smacks depended upon the skill, and often luck, of their crews to get them in and out of the harbor safely. Since that time, however, two lighthouses have been built at Morgan Point, one in 1831, the other in 1868.

. . .

The original lighthouse built in 1831 was a white circular granite tower separated from the keeper's dwelling by 80 feet. It was located a few feet from the present building built in 1868, and its foundations are still there. In dry weather the outline of the circular tower may be distinctly seen. The whale oil for the light was kept in a separate brick house, parts of which are still in use.

. . .

Mrs. Daboll's eldest daughter used to help her mother tend the light. Legend has it that when winter storms raged and the girl had to leave her warm home to clean

the wicks at the lighthouse 80 feet away, she used to sing at the top of her voice to keep up her courage, startling mariners who passed by on such unfortunate nights.

. . .

About 1850, Captain Silas Spicer became the new keeper of the light. A single lamp was installed in place of the old ten lamps, and a more refined oil used to keep the wicks clean for a longer time. In the winter, when snow and hail packed itself against the glass of the lantern, Spicer had the difficult task, as did other keepers of other lights, of keeping the glass clear during heavy storms.

. . .

Lightkeepers were required to keep a record of all vessels which passed their lighthouse and had to submit the records to the federal government. In one year, Spicer recorded almost 400 schooners which passed at the light until the outbreak of the Civil War in 1861.

. . .

The fourth keeper of the light, a Mr. Barber, succeeded Spicer in 1861 and served until 1867. In that year, the Lighthouse Board decided to tear down the old tower built 30 years earlier and build a new lighthouse, combining in one building the tower and living quarters for the new keeper. The present building was completed and put in operation in 1868. The lenses of the new light were brought from Germany. The lamp burned lard oil instead of the old whale oil. The lard came in butts or barrels like ordinary lard. Before it could be put into the lamp, it had to be heated so that it would not congeal after it was put into the lamp. Late in the 19th century, a benzine or kerosene lamp was installed. It was said to have 2,000 candlepower and to give out a light that could be seen for 20 miles.

. . .

In 1922, the lighthouse was discontinued in favor of an automatic electric beacon erected on a foundation at the entrance to the channel of the Mystic River. This beacon was discontinued eventually in favor of a smaller one several years ago. The original iron beacon may now be seen at the entrance to the Noank Shipyard at the foot of Pearl Street in Noank.

. . .

The Morgan Point Lighthouse is one of several of the same type built by the federal government in the 1860's. Others are located on Block Island, Old Field Point, New

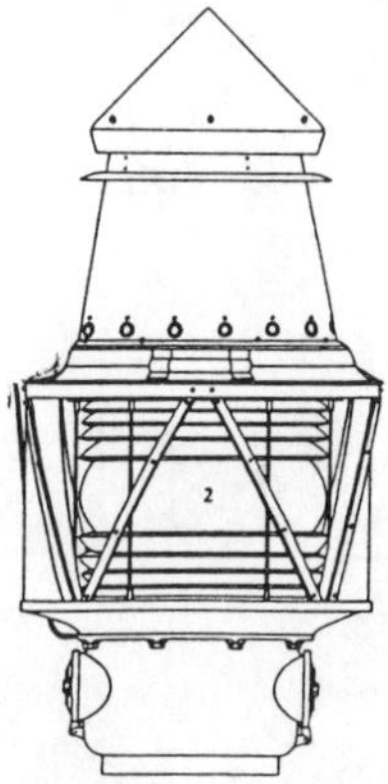

York and Great Captain Island, Greenwich, Connecticut. They were constructed of granite ashlar with extremely thick walls, approximately two feet, and all have slate gable roofs.

The wisdom of this solid construction is apparent 117 years later.

The lighthouse is in much of its original form, and practically no work has had to be done on its walls. Morgan Point Lighthouse survived the devastating hurricanes of 1938, 1944 and 1985, as well as the many storms of the 1950's without difficulty. In the 1938 hurricane, everyone on the Point went to the lighthouse as the one safe place to be.

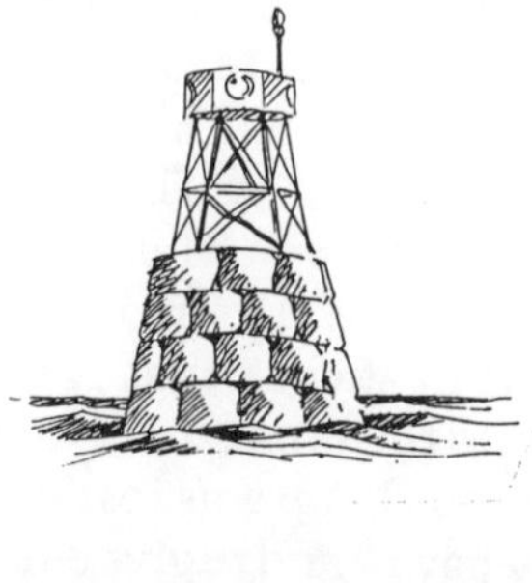

Rescuing the Depot

19a

The first big step toward refurbishing the village's train station will be taken Saturday.

Members of Mystic Depot Inc. have planned Depot Day — an afternoon of music, children's activities, souvenir sales and speech-making —to begin an effort aimed at raising $30,000 toward renovation of the depot.

Beginning at 11 a.m., the 35-piece New London Whalers Band will welcome incoming Amtrak trains and serve as a background for raising a large simulated locomotive steam gauge on which contributions will be registered.

"Substantial" contributions have been received from the Mystic Rotary, Mystic Seaport, the Marinelife Aq-

uarium, Olde Mistick Village, the Mystic Chamber of Commerce and Whaler Enterprises.

Mystic Depot, a non-profit group formed to head the renovation campaign, plans to refurbish the interior and exterior of the 70-year old building. The parking lot will be resurfaced and the area will be landscaped with the help of the Mystic Garden Club.

The exterior design of the building, which has been used as a model for Lionel model train stations, will remain the same, but the interior will be rearranged to make room for office space to be leased to several tenants.

The cost of the entire job, including plumbing, heating, electrical work and roofing, is estimated at about $75,000.

Amtrak, which owns the station, will pay $45,000 of the costs as part of a program to upgrade small stations in cooperation with local communities.

Waterborne

20

Celebrities

During the summer the Mystic River is polluted with a steady procession of plastic power boats. On Sundays one gets away from his dock with the peril of drivers entering a freeway. Since there is no break in the traffic, one simply picks something small and barges out. Some of these passing boats contain celebrities. Burl Ives, the folkish singer, arrived one Sunday in a cabin cruiser to "go to church" in what one boatyard owner described as "bare, dirty feet." Gary Moore, the TV Personality, has passed in his Kute Tug *Little Toot*; the two big coups, however, were first the arrival of Ted Kennedy and family on a large sailing vessel just after brother Robert's assassination (the Kennedys were trying to escape) and in 1969 Frank Sinatra's *Roma*. Teen-agers flocked to the highway bridge and screamed, "We want Frank" and he stepped out onto the deck and obliged them with a wave.

Innocence

After work I went across the bascule to where they'd docked, and watched the crew, many in beards, at the time exotic. The next day I brought my father down to the dock. It was the first time he'd been out of the house and since he had always loved schooners I thought it would be a good occasion to celebrate. He walked carefully over to the edge of the pier and, leaning against a pile, watched the crews of the two boats. They had

rafted facing downstream and seemed to take up half the river. With the four masts there was a great deal of rigging.

"Where are you going?" asked my father at last. A young man with a beard had caught us watching him scrape the deck.

"St. Thomas," said the young man. He said it with the kind of bland cheer which undermined even my confidence.

My father pulled at his mustache. "Pretty late, isn't it?"

"Oh no, it's very pleasant down there this time of year."

I expected my father to say something about the point being one had to get there before it was pleasant, but he seemed to consider a phrase, chew it, swallow it. That, he knew, was the kind of crack his father would have made. Yet the boy had to be told somehow. "Going to get some new running rigging here from Malcolm?"

"Some what?"

Again he bit his lip. Ended up waving his hand at the halyards and sheets. The young man looked up as if revealed to him were a bright tropic bird sitting upon the masthead; instead he found the raw autumn sky and settled for that.

"That's an. . . interesting furl you've got there," said my father. It was, of course, not executed properly.

"What?"

"The way you've got that foresail."

"We'll be in St. Thomas within a week."

The young man continued to scrape the deck. My

G

father continued to scrutinize the rigging. The wind blew gulls about like old newspapers, and my father, who did not like old newspapers, hunched his shoulders. "You're going to get it down in the City Island then."

"What's that?"

"The running rigging."

"We're jumping off right from here. This afternoon. Montauk Point."

"You're going *outside*?"

"This is a schooner."

I watched them go downriver the next day. From the office window across the shrouded power boats I saw their masts moving through snow flurries, an old newsreel, so that already they seemed passing into legend and later when in an old newspaper I found that the Coast Guard had come up with the hatch of one off Cape Henry it seemed only natural. The other made it to the Georges in Hamilton and the lifesavers were able to get her crew before she sank.

Interview

There may well need be a glossary of technical terms here for the sake of those who read as if they were filling out an accident report. While writing this section, I went back to McGugan's to check details and George told me of a problem he had had that morning. They had been hauling the dredge *Captain Frank* when one of the helpers slipped on the cradle and hurt his rib. They took him to the hospital, where George stood in for the interview.

"What kind of work does the firm do?"
"Marine contracting."
"You contact Marines?"
"Build things on water."
"You build things on water?"
"We try it."
"Try what?"
"Piers, pilings, catwalks and carpentry."
"The man was doing carpentry work on a piling?"
"He was actually on the railway."
"You work for the railroad?"
"*Marine* railway."
"You work for the government?"
"He fell off the cradle."
"How old did you say he was?"

20 Drifting

The current swept us out under the trestle, a clean maneuver unencumbered by memories of bats or anticipations of freights, and we popped into the lower estuary, Ram Island before us, the Noank waterfront to our right. After the shadow of the bridge, everything seemed much brighter.

We floated past Heathen Point, so named because at the height of Noank's orthodoxy, there had been a family living there which had not gone to church; past the site of the Old Bayside Hotel, now the graveyard of old lobster boats. Two were Noank style, sloop hulls modified with cutty cabin to one side like a phone booth. The other was the Novi or Maine model with a long, sweeping hull. It not only still had its outriggers, but they were in the trolling position as if from the moonlit spartina they might yet extract a flashing marlin.

Of the Noank models, one belonged to an old man who had been overcome by misfortune before he could get an engine in her; the other, prettiest of all, was a Noank sloop built in 1910 which was going to be restored by a mad wood-carver who wore a black beard and derby.

Past the yacht club, summer scene of signal flags, wild dresses and ginsprinkled spinnakers; past the shore dinner wharf, summer home of those whose fondest

A

delight is to digest endlessly; past the end of old Three-toed Alley, where once dozens of schooners lay drying sail, their gaffs scandalized, their decks adorned by cats with three toes; past the ruined piles of the MacDonald market, where they'd shipped fifty barrels of lobsters a day; past the old Spicer house, a farmhouse grown fat on sealing and then nuclear subs and now sporting a new veranda upon which in summer sat lacquered rattan chairs with hoods like cobras.

The moonlight spread out past the estuary into the Sound. It might have been August and we were hanging off the main dock a moment, the piles and islands suspended in classical Japanese brushwork.

Deep-Water Songs

21

These songs, traditional aboard deep-water square riggers, were sung not for work, like shanties, but for entertainment. Songs of this type were sometimes called "main-hatch songs," or, by the British, "fore-bitters." In the second dog-watch, from 6:00 to 8:00 P.M., the men usually gathered in clear weather around one of the hatches, or the forecastle head, and there was singing, and dancing of jig and hornpipe.

"There would perhaps be a man with an accordion in the middle of the hatch," said Captain Patrick Tayluer in a recorded interview. "He would strike up a familiar tune, and away all the sailors would sing it! The officers would often come down and join in the choruses. The cap'n, he would stand at the break of the poop, and smile and sing the choruses with the men, sometimes.

"These songs, they went around, all over the different ships, and the men would sing them so as to bring cheer to the watch that was going to have the eight hours out that night. Eight hours on deck of a nighttime is a mighty long time to a man! Four hours between eight and twelve, and four hours between four and eight. The four-and-eight watch was known very often as 'the death watch,' simply because most accidents at sea happened in the morning watch, the first watch of the day."

Songs of many kinds were popular at sea, created by sailormen and dealing with sailor life. There were "farewell songs"; songs of famous vessels and others not so famous; ballads of sea fights and piracy; songs of adventures ashore in Sailor Town.

The Leaving of Liverpool

I'm bound to California
By way of 'ol Cape Horn,
An' I bet that I will curse the day
An' the hour that I was born.

I've shipped in a Yankee clipper ship,
Davy Crockett is her name.
Captain Burgess he is tough, me lads,
And the mate he's just the same.

'Tis me second passage with ol' Burgess
An' I think I knows him well.
If a man's a sailor, he can get along,
But if not, he's sure in hell.

Fare-ye-well to Lower Frederick Street,
Anson Place, and Parkee Lane,
'Tis a long, long time, me bucko boys,
Ere I see you all again.

So fare-ye-well my own true love,
Goodbye, my love, goodbye.
'Twill be a long, long time, my dear,
But my darlin' don't ye cry.

Through the great seaport on the Mersey passed most of the trade between the United Kingdom and the Americas. Thousands of Yankee shellbacks knew Liverpool well. Many of the famous American clippers, too, were familiar sights in the Mersey, among them the three-skysail-yarder *David Crockett* of New York. Her figurehead now hangs in the Marine Museum at Mystic, Connecticut, where she went down the ways in 1853. The *David Crockett* often called at Liverpool on her passages homeward from California. It was in 1863 that she first arrived in the port while under command of Captain John A. Burgess of Massachusetts, her skipper for many years. In 1874, on what was to have been his last voyage before retiring from the sea, Captain Burgess was lost overboard in a storm in the South Atlantic.

Why Whales? 1c

Whale products were used for candles, whale oil lamps, cosmetics, buggy whips, canes, parasols, corset stays. And as the nation became industrialized, whale oil also filled the need for a fine lubricant. With the development and refinement of petroleum, however, the demand for whale oil decreased and the industry declined rapidly in this country.

On December 31, 1971, whaling and the importation of whale products by U.S. firms was prohibited in an effort to save this "fascinating mammal" from extinction.

Rumrunners I 22

It was, in fact, possible to believe almost anything about rumrunners. In the same month [August, 1924] U.S. Attorney Robert O. Harris in Boston said he had been informed that a big German submarine of commercial type was operating off Cape Cod and "flooding" the Cape area with foreign beer, ale, and wine. The story coincided with reports by airplane pilots in the New York area of unidentified submarines lying in the Hudson.

Customs agents at Mystic seized a former government one-man torpedo boat valued at $100,000. This craft, capable of carrying 400 cases of liquor and maintaining

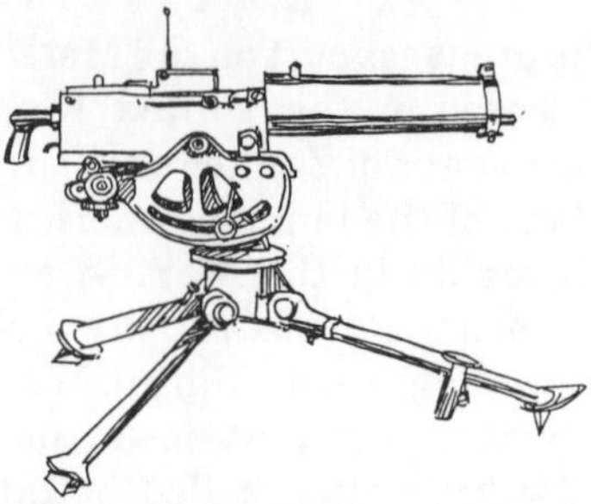

a speed of 33 knots, had 60 dabs of fresh gray paint covering dents in her armor that resembled bullet marks. It was believed that she was the vessel that two weeks before had tried to ram and sink the customs cutter *Shark* off Montauk. In the chase, the *Shark* had fired 800 machine-gun bullets at the craft she was pursuing.

12

Rumrunners II

One night a rum runner was almost caught just outside of the mouth of the Mystic River. To escape the Coast Guard boat that was in hot pursuit, the skipper headed his craft up the river. As he approached the railroad bridge he tooted his horn and yelled that it was an emergency and he had to get through. The bridge was opened for him and he made a run for the nearest shipyard. He told the man on duty that his craft had sprung a leak and was in danger of sinking and could he be hauled out immediately. The man obliged and hauled him up on the ways and into the shed and closed the doors. While the unsuspecting men of the shipyard looked for the leak, the Coast Guard ship was cruising up and down the river wondering what had happened to the elusive rum runner (so the story was told).

Logs and Journals

41

The terms 'logbook' and 'journal' are used interchangeably and even whalemen themselves sometimes referred to the official logbook as 'a journal of the voyage'. Although not always distinguishable, each has distinct differences.

A logbook was the official record of a voyage kept only by the mate; a journal was a personal record kept by a master, an officer or any member of the crew.

A whaling logbook was a record of a business venture in which a large sum was invested. In a sense, it was a report of an executive to his corporation. It gave the owners and agent a means of evaluating the master's handling of the vessel, his success in obtaining oil and the extent to which he was economical in the use of provisions. Being an official record of a voyage, it became the property of the whaling company at the end of the voyage.

Typical day by day entries provide pretty dull reading and only occasionally is the dullness relieved by something eventful. The monotony of a logbook simply reflects the monotony with which one day followed another. Whalemen faced hardship and danger so often that even the logbook entries describing them were casual and off-hand.

H

The following is a typically dull entry taken verbatim from the logbook of the ship *Charles Drew*.

Sunday, Nov. the 28th (1847)

These 24 hours commences with a moderate breese from the S.S.E. steering W.N.W. and cloudy weather at sunset took in sail steering W by N with a moderate breese middle and latter part pleasant weather at 5 AM made all sail steering W by N at 10 AM steering N by W.

These terse entries recorded essential information about the course, wind direction and intensity, weather conditions and the latitude and longitude if sights were taken. Occasionally other information was recorded concerning the sails used, landfalls, vessels sighted or gammed, whales sighted or captured, sickness of the crew (this off-duty time was deducted at the end of the voyage), accidents, deaths, desertions, misdemeanors, mutinies, punishment meted out and storms and damage sustained by the vessel. Various ship's duties involving the working and repair of the vessel, breaking out provisions, cutting-in whales,

trying out oil and bundling bone were also reported.

On a voyage of several years duration it was rare, if ever, for the vessel to return with the same officers and crew. Desertions were common, promotions were made to fill vacant posts and transfers to other vessels occurred because of illness or promotion. Thus, it was not unusual to find the handwriting change several times in a logbook.

Whaling logbooks and journals are often adorned with illustrations of three kinds: pencil or pen and ink sketches, watercolor illustrations and wood-block impressions. Seldom is the work of a genuine artist found but the intrinsic value of a manuscript is heightened by their presence and even crude sketches help to relieve the monotony of the daily entries. They are also important because they convey impressions made by contemporary observers.

Among the manuscripts there are illustrations of vessels, landfalls, harpoons, lances, whales, fish, turtles, flags, signals, maps, plants, boats after whales, the cutting-in process, anchorages, sails, spars, native

boats, compass roses, the method of stowing casks, islands in the South Shetlands, coral reefs, jagging wheels, the Mexican War and domestic scenes reflecting the work of homesick whalemen.

In the few articles written on the subject of scrimshaw, no mention is made of the wooden stamps carved by whalemen to decorate the pages of many logbooks and journals. The flat relief surface of the block was inked and stamped beside the appropriate entry on the page.

Impressions may be found throughout logbooks and journals of sperm and right whales, whale flukes, blackfish, porpoises, anchors, whaleboats, turtles and a stamp of a man holding a spyglass which appears in the journal of the ship *Richard Mitchell.*

Many logbooks contain one or more pages of whale stamps representing a record of whales seen or captured or by whom sighted. The latter was for the payment of a bounty to the sharp-eyed seaman who sighted the whale.

. . .

"The whaling interests of the country keeps in continual occupation a fleet of 600 sail, manned by 15,000 American seamen - which fishes up annually from the depths of the ocean, property, the real value of which far exceeds that of the gold mines of California."

I

8c

Nothing Worth of Remarks

Sunday September 7th [1851] Commences with fresh winds from the SSW with clear weather Ship under main top gallant sail by a wind to the SE the Island of St. Mary in Sight Barring NE Dist 20 miles Saw a barke cruising at 7 p Spoak the Barque Hellin Snow of newbedford 50 Days out Cleere middle part Squaley attended with heavy rain wind baffaling from S to SW. Latter part fresh winds from the SW with clear weather Ship by a wind to the SSE. Saw nothing worth of remarks So Ends Lat by obs. 36°08 North Long by Chro 24°12 West.

8d

Shipyard and Ships

In 1853 a shipyard was established in West Mystic by William E. Maxson, Capt. N.G. Fish, Capt. William Clift, B.F. Hoxie and William Barber under the name of Maxson, Fish and Co. This yard was on the Mystic River, below the railroad bridge and on the site of the present West Mystic Shipyard. At the outbreak of the Civil War these gentlemen, with the exception of Maxson and Capt. Fish, retired, but the yard continued the active construction of vessels.

Among the ships built by Maxson and Fish before the war were the *F.G. Hoxie*, 1387 tons in 1854 and the *Aspasia*, 632 tons in 1856. These ships are considered "Clippers".

During the war the yard built fourteen steamers, among them the *Galena*, the first iron-clad in the U.S. Navy, designed by Samuel H. Pook.

In 1865 two steamers were sold to a Boston firm, the *Casandra* for $103,000 and the *Augusta* for $185,000 to be used as freighters on the Boston, New Orleans run.

During the decade of the 1860's the yard also built five "Half Clippers" or "Down Easters", among which were the *Seminole*, the *Helicon* and the *Dauntless*. These ships were less extreme than the true Clippers built in the 1850's, but had greater carrying capacity and a good turn of speed.

Capt. Fish lived on the "New London Road", the present route 1, on the corner of West Mystic Avenue, and during his later years owned and ran a Ship Chandlery on Water Street, in Mystic, under the name of N. G. Fish & Co. The Ship Chandlery at the Mystic Sea-

port Museum is a reconstruction of his store. A

The diaries, which have been in the possession of his family, are for 1855, when he was active at the busy shipyard, and the year 1868 when most of his time was given to the store and to his other interests.

The First Ironclad

8d

The *Galena* was launched at the Maxson and Fish Shipyard on February 14, 1862. She was constructed in 130 days, including the installation of her iron plating which was 2 to 4 inches thick. She was commissioned on Apr. 21, 1862 and was classed as a third rate screwsteamer, 738 tons, with four nine inch Dahlgren guns and two 100 pound Parrott rifles. She had cost the government $247,284.40. On May 15 she attempted, in company with the *Monitor* and 3 small gunboats, to subdue the Confederate battery at Drewry's Bluff on the James River and open the water route to Richmond, Va. Unfortunately her armor proved insufficient to withstand the fire from the battery and she was forced to withdraw with severe damage, and thirteen killed and eleven wounded. She was subsequently stripped of her armor plate and took a gallant part in Farragut's Battle at Mobile Bay. She served in the U.S. Navy until 1891.

23 Noank Sloop/Packet

Noank was quite isolated in 1825. That was the year that Deacon Robert Palmer was born. There were only 13 houses in the little village at that time, although it soon came to be a rapidly growing community. Since the roads were hardly more than cart-paths, and exceedingly difficult to travel, it was necessary that in order to establish any contact with the outside world, transportation by water must be the means employed.

This situation demanded a type of vessel which could accommodate passengers and at the same time provide facilities for carrying freight. Necessity has always been the mother of invention and soon the resourceful shipbuilders along the Mystic River developed a sloop-rigged vessel which seemed to meet the requirements.

These packets, so called because of the use for which they were intended, were the forerunners of larger fishing fleets and were a radical departure from the smaller clinker-built smackees then in common use. While there was always some variation, in general these sloops were about 55 feet long in overall measurement, had an 18 foot beam and a 7 foot draught. The rig consisted simply of a mainsail, jib and a jib-staysail which was for use in light weather. The ten berths in the cabin were shared by both the crew and the passengers, while the space forward provided room in which generous shipments of supplies could be placed. There were three packet lines operated from Mystic and Noank to New York.

MENSURATION.

If the vessel be double-decked, take the length thereof from the fore-part of the main stem to the after part of the stern-post above the upper deck; the breadth thereof at the broadest part above the main wales, half of which breadth shall be accounted the depth of such vessel; then deduct from the length three-fifths of the breadth, multiply the remainder by the breadth, and the product by the depth; divide this last product by ninety-five, and the quotient will be the true content or tonnage of such vessel.

If the vessel be single-decked, take the length and breadth as above directed, in respect to a double-decked vessel, and deduct from the length three-fifths of the breadth, and taking the depth from the under side of the deck plank to the ceiling of the hold; multiply and divide as aforesaid, the quotient will be the true content or tonnage of such vessel.

Carpenters, in finding the tonnage, multiply the length of the keel by the breadth of the main beam and the depth of the hold in feet, and divide the product by 95; the quotient is the number of tons. In the double decked vessels half the breadth is taken for the depth.

Gunkholing

Noank, Connecticut (13214). This village, on the west bank of the Mystic River, has docks along the waterfront, with plenty of deep water. But don't get too close to nuns 8 or 10. The well-kept Noank Shipyard, located behind a protected bulkhead on the port shore just above nun 8, is the first facility you'll reach and as such offers as complete service as you'll find anywhere, including emergency repair work of all types with mechanics, carpenters, and riggers on duty seven days a week. It provides its customers with gas, diesel fuel, ice, water, an excellent marine store with charts, showers, a 60-ton Travelift, and moorings for transients. They can be reached at (203) 536-9651 or over VHF-16. A laundromat and a store for supplies is nearby. The *Bill of Rights*, a deep-draft, 125 foot schooner, is a frequent visitor here.

For those vessels which are not over 40 feet, have no advance reservations at Mystic Seaport, and may not wish to make the long trek up the Mystic River, a layover is suggested at Spicer's Noank Marina in West Cove, west of Morgan Point. Make your approach to this expanding facility by heading north between can 1 and the red-and-green buoy "S" making sure to give Mouse Island as shown on the chart a fairly wide berth

to starboard. Then head for the daybeacons set out by the marina marking the approach channel recently dredged to 7 feet MLW. Spicer's anchorage area, outside their new breakwater, is patrolled by its launch which monitors VHF-9 and runs from 8 A.M. to 9 P.M. daily. One may reserve an overnight slip in 7 foot depths by checking in at Spicers gas dock and marine store.

This full service marina offers the visitor several advantages. A variety of stores for supplies are easily reached by a short walk to Noank. Mystic Seaport is only a ten minute cab ride away, and the Sea Horse Restaurant is conveniently located by the floating docks unexposed to the Mystic River traffic.

Just beyond Noank Shipyard stands one of Noank's major assess, Abbott's, the largest lobster pound in southern New England. Visitors come here from miles around to tie up dockside while ordering fresh clams, shrimp, or lobster for instant eating on the porch outside or to be taken aboard.

Upriver, just beyond nun 12, you'll note the long, sturdy-looking dock of the Ram Island yacht Club. There is a flagpole on the pier. This modest-sized club has 4 1/2 feet at MLW off this pier, few services for transients, but does have a possible guest mooring available.

In ordinary summer weather, Noank is OK for overnight, but it is very exposed to winds from the northeast to southeast, and is close to the much-used channel to Mystic Seaport, thus a victim to the wash of many passing boats. To the southeast of nun 12, transient yachts may anchor in the area just to the south of the special anchorage noted on the chart. But although it gives shelter from winds out of the east, only 5 feet MLW is recorded and the soft bottom here provides poor holding ground.

Mason Island, Connecticut (13214). Progress has come to Mason Island, so far as facilities for yachtsmen are concerned. On the west shore of Mason Island, opposite black can 23, is a fine, classy, modern marina, the Mystic River Marina, with 8 feet in the slips at low water and a reported 10 or 12 feet at the end of the gas dock. Here, besides gas and diesel fuel, are available many slips, water, ice, electricity, showers, toilets, telephone, laundromat, marine store, swimming pool, restaurant, a mechanic on duty, and a 20-ton Travelift.

On the other side of the island, with less luxury and more privacy, there is an anchorage between Mason and Dodges islands off the flagstaff of the Mason Island Yacht Club, which has a pier on the east shore of Mason Island Yacht Club, just north of Enders Island. Visiting yachtsmen from other recognized yacht clubs are welcomed at this attractive club, located on the private property of the Mason Island Company.

Ten feet can be carried 100 yards north of the flagstaff. There is excellent holding ground and plenty of room to swing, but the place is not too good in a blow, as it is open to the south and has a long sweep to the north also. On the way up to this secluded, attractive anchorage, be sure to leave nun 6 well to starboard to avoid the rocks to the northwest.

In northerlies, better protection can be found by running around Enders Island into the bright between there and Mason Point.

Mystic, Connecticut (13214). Entering the Mystic River, you see the picturesque village of Noank to port, where a floodlit church spire is a beacon after dark,

and off your starboard quarter Mason Island and the Mystic River marina. The course is nearly due north to Mystic, at the upper end of which is the Marine Historical Association's far-famed maritime museum, Mystic Seaport. A near-perfect shelter for visiting yachtsmen, amid attractive surroundings, aesthetic as well as history laden, is offered here.

The railroad bridge has a flexible schedule, governed, of course, by the flow of traffic over its rails. If a train is approaching, you must wait in the river until it passes. While waiting, look just beyond the bridge to the left of the rocky promontory, partially covered by foliage, with a few old houses strewn about its base. This was Fort Rachel, where in 1814 a hardy band of local people successfully manned an artillery battery and soundly repulsed the British, who were bent to the task of the assault and sack of the town.

Concerning your passage upriver, we add the following words of caution: The speed limit throughout the river is 6 miles per hour; this limit is posted and enforced. The average river channel depth at mean low water is about 12 feet. However, there is serious shoaling in many spots, especially at the channel turns. So beware of the pitfalls of the Mystic River channel!

Since there is little sense in going through the bascule bridge into the Mystic Seaport unless you have a confirmed reservation, and since anchoring in the channel is obviously prohibited, the unexpected visitor must have an alternative plan. One time we put in at the floating slips of the Whit-Mar Marina, located just to the east of nun 30 on Murphy Point. Although the depth at the slips has been dredged to 5 feet at low water, this marina does not accommodate boats over 40 feet... In approaching or leaving, be sure to stay south of the pilings standing off the north side of the dock. The services are adequate here and it is less congested than at the facilities further upriver.

West of nun 26, four deep-water docks belonging to the Mystic Shipyard stretch out into the river from Willow Point. This claims to be one of the east coast's finest yacht yards catering mainly to sailing craft. They provide full repair service and practically every other accommodation except fuel and a restaurant.

As you proceed upriver, you will find that the new

railroad swing bridge is usually open, but if it is closed, the bridge tender can be called on VHF-13/16. Just beyond this bridge on the east shore is located Seaport Marine which because of the 17-foot depth there, can berth vessels up to 100 feet.

A 1985 *Notice to Mariners* gives us this new regulation covering the operation of the next bridge you will meet, a bascule type [*bascule*, in French, means *seasaw*] on Route 1. "It shall open on signal, with a maximum delay of 20 minutes except: From May 1 through October 31 from 7:15 A.M. to 7:15 P.M., the draw need only open hourly at quarter past the hour." This bridge monitors VHF-16...

Advance reservations must be made for all visits to Mystic Seaport. These may be arranged by writing, or by telephoning and asking for the dockmaster on any day between 8:30 A.M. and 5 P.M. in season. All this should be done at least three weeks in advance of your planned arrival... Phone reservations are taken beginning in late April with mail reservations accepted starting in February. A $25 deposit, refundable upon 24-hour notice of cancellation, must accompany all requests.

When you arrive at the Seaport you will be met, at least between 8 A.M. and 7 P.M. by a dock attendant who will assist in your berthing, register you, and generally be at your service. He will deliver various folders that will help orient you, explain the museum exhibits, and answer questions relative to the shower and laundry facilities at the New York Yacht Club Station 10 Annex. He will also point the way to the Galley, the delightful Seamen's Inne, and the Seaport Stores. At the dock houses adjacent to the wharves, you will find weather information, tide tables, a list of local boat yards, and the taxi number. It is handy also to know that food markets and sprit shops are within easy walking distance of the Seaport.

(Visiting mariners should consult up to date sources for navigation on the Mystic River. For safety and convenience this description should NOT be relied upon.)

Qui se occupatum tenere vult has duas res armet: navem et mulierem. Nulla duae res quidem, aliquando ornatae, plus negotiorum continent. Neque hae satis ornantur, neque his nimis ornamentarum satis est.

--Titus Maccius Plautus
A. U. C. DLIII

(Translation page 177)

War and Peace

24

The Pequots

When Adrian Block, a Dutch navigator, explored our sea-coast in 1614, the Pequot and Mohegan Indians were located in the same places that they occupied in 1633, when our State was first settled by the English.

The Pequots were governed by a powerful sachem, whom they idolized and regarded "as all one god." Under his leadership they had become a terror to the neighboring tribes, with whom they had frequently been engaged in deadly hostilities.

The various tribes and clans tributary to the Pequots hailed the coming of the white man as an omen that foreshadowed their release from the tyranny of Sassacus. The Connecticut River Indians made the first effort to secure an alliance with the Massachusetts and Plymouth colonies.

In the year 1631 an Indian Sachem by the name of Wah-qui-ma-cut visited the Governors of the Plymouth and Massachusetts colonies, and offered them strong inducements to come and settle in the beautiful valley of the Connecticut, and proposed that two men should be delegated to view the country and report to the Governors. Governor Winthrop declined the offer; but Governor Winslow, of Plymouth, held the matter under consideration, and soon after visited the place, and on his return home gave a glowing description of its fertility, which tempted many a Puritan to leave his sterile home at Plymouth and explore this Indian paradise from the mouth of the river far back towards its sources.

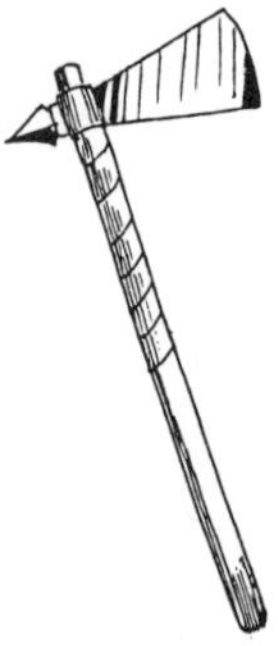

Meantime the shrewd and active Pequots were watching with sleepless vigilance the movements of the Plymouth people, doubtless foreseeing the danger that would result to them from a settlement of the

English upon the Connecticut River, and sought to counteract and prevent it by an alliance with the Dutch; for as early as 1632 they sold lands at Saybrook to the Dutch Governor at New Amsterdam.

. . .

For a long time previous to the coming of the English, Uncas and the Mohegans had been subject to the Pequots. They had made four attempts to secede and establish an independent tribe, but failed; but as soon as the English had commenced their settlement on the Connecticut River, Uncas with his adherents seceded and joined the Connecticut River Indians, in the vicinity of Hartford and Windsor, who had previously invited the planters to come and settle among them.

The failure of the Pequots to make a satisfactory treaty with the English, who had restored the Connecticut River Indians to their rightful territory and ousted the Dutch from the land sold them by the Pequots, and finally had sided with and sheltered Uncas, the arch rebel, who had so often defied them, was too much for the proud, warlike Pequots to endure; so they resolved to extirpate the English, not by a bold, manly effort, but by cutting them up piecemeal, with fire and torture the most diabolical and inhuman.

So when the General Court assembled they [the English] declared war, offensive war, against the Pequots, and raised an army of ninety men to invade the territory of the most warlike and cruel of all the New England tribes, and appointed Capt. John Mason commander-in-chief of the expedition. The soldiers were enlisted, equipped, and provisioned in ten days, and sailed from Hartford May 10, 1637, accompanied by Uncas and seventy friendly Indians. The fleet consisted of three vessels, and the English, being unacquainted with the navigation of the river, ran their vessels aground several times, but after five days they reached Saybrook Fort.

His little fleet lay wind-bound near the mouth of the river until the 18th, during which time Mason summoned and held a council of war, which decided to change the order of the General Court, and set sail for Narragansett Bay. They left Friday morning, and reached there Saturday evening, but were not able to land on account of the weather before the next Tuesday evening, May 23d, when they set out for the residence of Miantonomoh.

Mason marched the next morning, May 24th, for the Pequot fort. As he proceeded he was joined by a large party of Narragansetts sent on by Miantonomoh.

He reached the Niantic fort the next evening, which he surrounded until morning, when, after a fatiguing march of twelve miles, he reached the fording-place on Pawcatuck River, when Mason and his army halted and rested. After dinner they marched on to Taugwonk, in Stonington, where they found a field just planted with Indian corn; here they halted and held another council of war. Mason learned that the Pequots had two forts, both of which were very strong. At first it was decided to attack both, but after learning that the one where Sassacus commanded was too remote to be reached in time, they resolved to go ahead and attack the fort at Mystic.

Their line of march all the way from Narragansett [Bay] had been along the old Indian path, traveled from time immemorial by the natives, until they crossed Pawcatuck River and reached Taugwonk, but from Taugwonk onward they deployed to the north, to avoid being discovered by the Pequots at Mystic fort, and at early evening they reached a place now known as Porter's Rocks, in Groton, where between two high ledges "they pitched their little camp." The night was clear, with a shining moon, and after Mason had set his guards he and his men lay down and slept. About two hours before day the men were called and ordered to get ready, and after commending themselves to the

keeping of the all-wise Disposer of events they set out for the fort, which was about two miles off.

There were two entrances to the fort, and it was decided that Mason should enter on the northeast side and Underhill [John Underhill from the Saybrook garrison] on the southwest side. Mason went forward, and when within a rod of the fort was discovered by a Pequot, who cried out, "Owanux! Owanux!"

Mason and his men entered the fort through the northeast passage, while Underhill and his men passed in at the southwest. A hand-to-hand contest ensued on both sides of the fort. Mason soon saw that his only hope of complete success lay in burning their fort and wigwams, and immediately set fire to them which spread with wonderful rapidity. The scene which followed was awful beyond all human description, the result of which was the complete overthrow of the Pequots as a tribe, and the consequent salvation of the English settlement on the Connecticut River. It was the most fearful chastisement that any tribe of Indians ever received; but when we consider the terrible cruelties perpetrated by them, the awful tortures that they inflicted upon their English captives, who shall say that justice did not overtake them?

. . .

After two hundred and thirty-nine years since the conquest of Mason, only a small remnant remains of the once powerful and haughty Pequots. No one can defend the horrible tortures that they inflicted upon the English who fell into their hands as prisoners. Their overthrow by Mason humbled their pride, and so far subdued them that ever afterwards they were the friends of the English. They joined our forces in King Phillip's war, and in the Great Swamp fight in 1675 performed prodigies of valor under Gallup and Avery. During the French war they voluntarily joined the expeditions that were raised to repel the invasion of the French and northern Indians.

But who can successfully defend all of the acts of the English towards the Pequots, especially after they had

yielded to their authority and became subservient to their power? It is not to be wondered at that the English failed in their efforts to Christianize the Pequots.

The commissioners of the United Colonies and nearly all of the clergymen of New England made praiseworthy efforts to afford the Indians religious instruction. But, after all, the treatment that the Pequots received from the authorities acting under the colonies of Connecticut and Rhode Island in the assignment of lands for their benefit and in other matters was so unjust and oppressive that it well nigh outweighed every consideration that was urged upon them by Elliott and his co-workers to effect their conversion and make them believe in the white man's God.

Most of the Pequot warriors preferred the favor of their Good Spirit Kritchian, and died believing that in the beautiful southwest land were hunting-grounds of boundless extent and game of endless variety, where no Hobomoke could charm the arrow from its fatal plunge nor mar their happiness in the Indian's summerland.

Indian Cure for the Ear-Ache.—Take a piece of the lean of mutton, about the size of a large walnut, put it into the fire, and burn it for some time, till it becomes reduced almost to a cinder; then put it into a piece of clean rag, and squeeze it until some moisture is expressed, which must be dropped into the ear as hot as the patient can bear it.

Fort Finding

15b

Kevin A. McBride is not the first archaeologist with dreams of finding what is left of the Pequot Indian fort that colonial soldiers burned in 1637.

"Archaeologists have looked for remains of the fort before, but no one has found it," McBride said Monday. "They might not have been looking for the right things."

With hopes of locating the remains, McBride plans an excavation that will begin this May [1987] on the west bank of the Mystic River.

The search will start at the John Mason statue in Groton, across the water from Mystic Seaport.

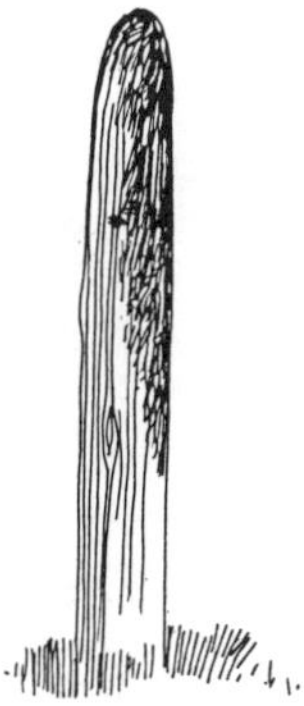

It is not surprising that remains of the fort have not been found, according to McBride. "These things are really hard to see. What would remain would not be very obvious," he said. Scattered mounds of buried trash and artifacts and maybe the remnants of burnt posts are what he hopes to find.

. . .

Coastal areas such as Bluff Point State Park and Noank where Pequots lived following the 1637 massacre, will be important in the Groton survey.

Research will begin this winter. "We will question what people are finding in the area. Sometimes when digging gardens or putting in roadways, people find things. We might get lucky that way," he said.

The artifacts will be near the surface, he said. "Probably no more than 18 inches, two feet at the most."

14a

Privateers
(Revolutionary War)

The privateers were another matter. History has paid too little attention to their role in the struggle for independence. Yet they did great damage to British shipping. These privately-owned vessels armed and manned at the owner's expense, cruised offshore to capture enemy merchantmen. They carried a commission of "letter-of-marque" from the Continental Congress. This authorization kept them within the law and removed from piracy. Vessels sized by privateers were "prizes;" after being condemned in port by due process of law they could be sold and the proceeds divided among the owner, officers and crew.

The Continental Navy was but a token force, and the privateers prizes helped supply weapons for the war. A bloody tale is told about the Mystic privateer *Eagle*,

whose captain, Edward Conkling, was a refugee from British raids on Long Island. On a single day in May 1779 the *Eagle* took so many prizes that most of her crew of 30 left to sail the captured ships to port. British sailors imprisoned aboard the *Eagle* soon out-numbered the Americans. They killed Conkling and his men, four of them from Groton. The mate, aboard one of the prizes, was a horrified witness, but could do nothing to prevent the murders.

25

Defense
The War of 1812

West Mystic bristles all over with stern granite crags, on which and amid which the houses of the village nestle. On one of these, commanding the ship channel, and some forty feet above it, stood Fort Rachel, one of the defenses of Mystic in the war of 1812.

A friend who accompanied us thither for a Sunday evening stroll told its story as follows.

"In the war of 1812, as you know, the British paid much more attention to this part of the coast than to any other, several of their larger vessels patrolling our waters almost constantly. On the 12th of June, 1813, an armed cutter of the enemy, with a launch in tow, was seen approaching up the ship channel yonder, with the evident design of plundering and burning the town, as he had several of our coast villages. A masked battery of one twelve-pounder, named Fort Rachel, after a local heroine, had already been thrown up on this rock, which, as you see, commands the ship channel completely. An express hastily summoned the minute-

men of the village to the fort, which was unmanned. Twenty men responded. There was powder for the gun, but no ball, but spikes, scrap iron and pieces of chain were hastily gathered and thrust into the muzzle. The British, quite unsuspicious of danger, were allowed to approach to about where the drawbridge now stands, when the gun was fired at point-blank range, sweeping the cutter's decks. As soon as she could recover from the confusion the cutter manned her launch, and sent a detachment ashore to carry the cliff, which, to appearance, was undefended; but while this was being done, our lads, under Captain Haley, had time to load, and as the launch neared the shore again discharged their weapon with such good judgment that the craft was sent to the bottom, and most of her men were killed or wounded. The British commander then turned and fled. In plundering and burning houses tenanted by defenseless women and children he had been measurably successful, but for

contending against spikes and scrap iron he had no stomach.

"This Haley, with four other Mystic men - Burrows, Park, Washington and Tufts - was the hero of another gallant affair. For two days after Hardy* attacked Stonington, the British fleet lay off the Hummocks, and our boys thought they would try a stratagem on them. They manned a large sloop-rigged fishing boat, loaded her with boxes, barrels and bags, and sailed out past the fleet as if intending to run the blockade. Meantime, one looking through the hill yonder might have seen Capt. Jonathan Wheeler's company of Groton militia concealing themselves amid the rocks of Groton Long Point. The British eagerly pursued the American sloop in the familiar barge used in their predatory excursions. The sloop at first tried to outsail her pursuers, but apparently failing in the attempt, turned and ran in upon Groton Long Point, where the men beached her and fled on shore. The British eagerly pursued them, and when once on land were met by a volley from the militia, which killed several, wounded more, and sent the survivors into the water, where they surrendered. The captured barge was afterwards sold for $1,200, a part of the proceeds being divided among the captives."

*Admiral Sir Thomas Hardy, at this time aboard his flagship *Ramillies*, 75 gun frigate. Captain Hardy was in command of *Victory* at the Battle of Trafalgar in 1805. Ed.

G

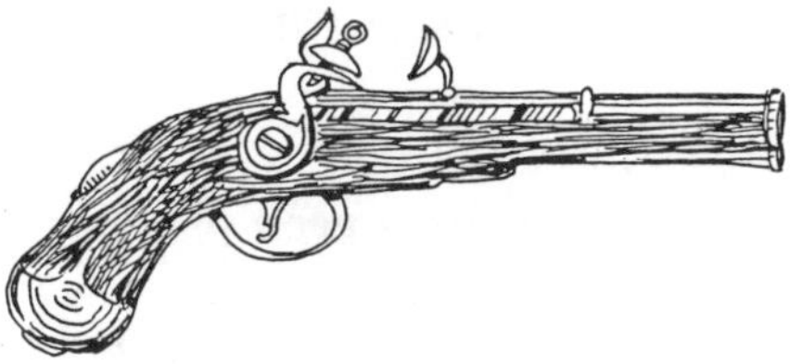

Retribution

23

In the early spring of 1813, a British fleet having a rendezvous at Block Island quite effectually closed Long Island Sound to all trading ventures. A few men, bolder than the others, attempted to run through the British lines. On one of these expeditions Captain Jesse Crary, in the sloop *Fox*, was captured. After a time Captain Crary succeeded in making his escape and finding his way home; he immediately began to make plans to recapture the *Fox* and to continue his raids upon the enemy fleet. Accordingly, the sloop *Hero* was fitted out as a privateer and, with a crew of Mystic and Noank men, she sailed from New London in search of the enemy.

They found the *Fox* cruising around Block Island, and a sharp encounter followed which ended in a hand-to-hand fight on the deck of the captured sloop. Finding themselves greatly outnumbered and also outclassed, the enemy crew surrendered and the *Hero* in an undamaged condition was able to bring her prize with the prisoners to a safe anchorage in the Mystic River.

10d

Aux Armes!

Editor of the Semi-Weekly:

Why would it not be a good plan for the town of Groton to appropriate $3,000 for the relief of the starving Cubans, and drop the proposed bicycle path? If this plan is not to be entertained, then spend the amount in repairing the road to Lantern Hill, in cutting down several of the bad grades and widening the highways. This second suggestion would please everyone as it would make the Hill more accessible in case the Spaniards invade the Valley.

Mainstreet

10b

Speak Up, Bucklyn!

Wednesday evening the streets of Mystic were alive with people eager to witness the celebration in honor of the arrival of Admiral George Dewey from Manila.

At 7:30 o'clock members of the [Dewey] club fired a salute of seventeen guns from an old mortar on Holmes' wharf. At every report the whistles on the mills and factories were blown and the noise was deafening. Firecrackers and rockets were set off, red fire was burned, and the Mystic Cornet Band enlivened the occasion by a concert on Hoxie House square. Capt. J. K. Bucklyn delivered an address from the balcony in front of the Opera House and his remarks were listened to by an audience of over one thousand people. Owing to the constant booming of the cannon and noise of the whistles and church bells his address could not be heard by all.

After the celebration, which lasted over an hour, the members of the Dewey club repaired to Cottrell's hall where a luncheon was served. The affair was very successful.

Institutions

Whipple's School

26

"About the year 1882 experiments were instituted in the Nebraska School for the Deaf at Omaha to ascertain whether hearing could be improved by use, and the startling discovery was made that children who at first appeared able to perceive little more than noise, could be trained, first to discriminate different kinds of noises (for example, the voice from the sound of a bell), and then distinctions of vocal effects (one vowel, for example, from another) until finally they became able to understand spoken utterance by hearing alone. This led to the Auricular Method of Instructing the Deaf...

"To Jonathan Whipple of Mystic belongs the honor of having first demonstrated auricular development in the deaf; and though the importance of the discovery was not understood or appreciated at the time - even by himself - we know it now. Had his results been investigated in a friendly, and impartial spirit, we would not have had to wait for twenty-three years for the establishment of the Oral Method in this country, and thirty-eight years for the Auricular Method." (Alexander Graham Bell, Hartford, March 1897)

. . .

Jonathan Whipple of Quakertown [now a part of Ledyard, Ct.] was destined by the birth of his son Enoch, who was born deaf circa 1826, to develop a strong creative interest in the deaf and how best to help his son and later others of similar impairment to communicate. A Herculean task confronted Jonathan. He was a man of meager education and had a total lack of knowledge pertaining to his son's condition.

One can only marvel at what he was able to accomplish in teaching Enoch to read lips and talk under such circumstances. Thought and patience, together with prayer, culminated in pioneering a method of teaching his son, who was not profoundly deaf, to attain the ability to read lips and talk. Initially, he was helped inadvertently by Enoch. He noted that the boy, when looking at a person speaking, would make repeated attempts to repeat a word. The thought occurred to him that perhaps every word had a shape,

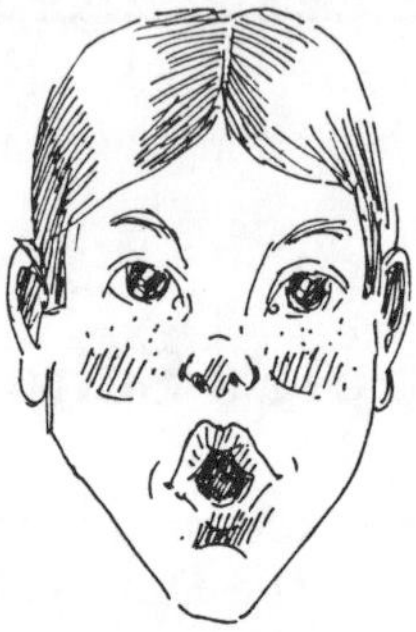

and by learning the shape of each letter, the boy might be taught to imitate it. Hand in hand with this reasoning on word shapes, he wondered if by constant repetition of speaking close to Enoch it would result in stimulating residual hearing and enable him to differentiate between sounds. The results he achieved attest conclusively to the merit of auricular instruction in developing latent auditory potential by the constant use of speech.

Available background material strongly tends to confirm that Jonathan was oblivious for many years of any previous success in teaching the deaf orally. In our country he was a pioneer in every sense of the word, the patriarch of the oral method of teaching. All in all, he was a remarkable man - one of spirit, courage and fidelity.

. . .

Zerah C. Whipple enters into our story at this juncture. A grandson of Jonathan and nephew of Enoch, he was fascinated and inspired by the accomplishments of both men. To Zerah it was a proud and wondrous thought that Uncle Enoch was able to communicate by word of mouth and that grandfather had made it possible. He knew a number of people who did business for years with his uncle and were not cognizant of his uncle's impairment.

It is not unreasonable to assume his regard for Grandfather Jonathan and Uncle Enoch created a desire which culminated in his decision to make teaching the deaf his life's work. At the time he was only nineteen years old. After considerable deliberation between Grandfather Whipple and himself, a decision was made in 1869 to start a school for the deaf in grandfather's house. It was to be known as the Whipple Home School for Deaf Mutes. Zerah became the first teacher and principal with the arrival in November of Willie S. Downing of Wilmington, Delaware, an eleven year old and the school's first student.

. . .

Accomplishments of the school during Zerah's tenure as principal were considerable. He invented the Whipple Natural Alphabet, a constructive aid in the developing methods of teaching the deaf.

. . .

Some three or four years after the school was started space became a problem [and] the school moved to its present location [in Mystic].

. . .

A decision reluctantly arrived at [1895] was the need for a new name for the school. The name Mystic Oral School for the Deaf was adopted. The change, it was hopefully felt would help overcome any onus attached to the former name.

Ed. Note: The State of Connecticut bought the school in 1921. It became a facility of the State Department of Education in 1959. In 1988, it's still referred to locally as "the oral school."

27

Recycling Portersville Academy

Portersville Academy, built by the Fifth School District in 1839, was first located just north of what is now known as the Union Baptist Church on High Street. The first schoolhouse was located just west of the church and had become too small to serve the approximately 100 children in the district. The new schoolhouse was built by Amos Clift at a cost of $1,365.95.

...

In 1887 the Town of Groton bought the building, which was no longer needed as a schoolhouse, for the "purpose of holding Town and Electors Meetings, the holding of Courts, and for any other purpose or purposes for which a Town Hall may properly and legally be used." The building was moved to its present site on

South High Street. It was used as the Town Hall of the First Voting District of the Village of Mystic River until 1958 when it was deserted and closed up.

In July 1966 the Groton Town council was reported in the *New London Day* to be ready to adopt a resolution directing the Public Works Department to demolish the old schoolhouse/town hall. It was saved by a group of concerned citizens and the now dissolved Mystic Valley Civic Association, which leased the building for $1 a year from the town. They worked extensively to save the exterior of the building, painting, repairing, and replacing window glass. The Mystic Garden Club graded and landscaped the lot.

When the Civic Association could no longer care for the building, it was again saved from demolition by the efforts of the Mystic Junior Women's Club. They also rented the building from the Town for $1 and paid for it to be insured. In 1974 the Mystic River Historical Society began efforts to acquire the old school-house; and in April 1975 the Town of Groton turned the property over to them. The Society plans to restore the schoolhouse and build a small adjacent building which will house and preserve the historical records, making them available to all persons interested in town history.

28

Among Other Things, an Aquarium

Mystic Marinelife Aquarium is a division of Sea Research Foundation, Inc., a nonprofit organization dedicated to public education and research. Its purposes are: to encourage a deeper appreciation for the dignity and uniqueness of aquatic animals; to help clarify man's position in nature and his effect on the aquatic environment; and to advance scientific knowledge of the aquatic world and the animals and plants inhabiting it.

B

28

MMA: Saving One

Mystic Marinelife Aquarium sends its rescue team to the aid of stranded imperiled marine mammals several times each year. These efforts are costly, exhausting and sometimes dangerous for the people involved, and always a gamble. Sometimes we know the exhilaration of beating the odds, as when we help return one member of an endangered species to the sea.

On The cold afternoon of March 12, two girls playing on rocks in Narragansett, RI, spotted a humpback

whale about 500 ft. off-shore. Drawn inshore to feed, apparently, it had become entangled in a line and was struggling to free itself. Alerted by the girls, the Coast Guard summoned the marine mammal rescue team from Mystic Marinelife Aquarium.

When Dr. J. Lawrence Dunn, the Aquarium vet, and trainers Curt Horton and Sandy Allen arrived in Narragansett that afternoon, it was already too dark to attempt a rescue and the water was too rough for their Mark II Zodiac, a small inflatable craft powered by an outboard engine. The next morning at eight o'clock the three began the rescue, aided by personnel from Rhode Island's Department of Environmental Management, who brought their vessel, *Gannett*, to the scene. The *Super Squirrel*, a private fishing boat, assisted as well by positioning itself to serve as a windscreen in the still-choppy and frigid water.

Outfitted with wet suits and SCUBA gear, Dunn, Allen and Harold Wes Pratt, a marine scientist with the National Marine Fisheries Service, cautiously swam around the struggling humpback. Measuring about 30 ft. and weighing somewhere between four and five tons, the whale had run afoul of two nylon lines attached to lobster pots. One line had coiled itself several times around the base of the tail, near the flukes. Dangling a few feet below the tail was a lobster pot and a styrofoam buoy. A second lobster pot hung about six

feet below the first. Another line, which the whale held in its mouth, had wrapped itself around the right pectoral fin. Trussed and weighted like this, the animal had drifted overnight to a point off Scarborough Beach.

(The humpback is a medium-size baleen whale described by Charles Scammon in 1874 as being "decidedly ugly, as it has a short thick body... with inordinately large pectorals and flukes." The pectorals of this species, easily one third the length of the body, are the largest pectorals found on any whale. Large knobs - callosities - on these long flippers, and on the whale's head and lower jaw, combine erratically with whitish encrustations of barnacles in the same areas to deprive the humpback of sleek beauty. But if its body is a cosmetic nightmare, its voice compels admiration, for this is the renowned singer of the deep, the basso profundo that literally fills the sea with its song. That

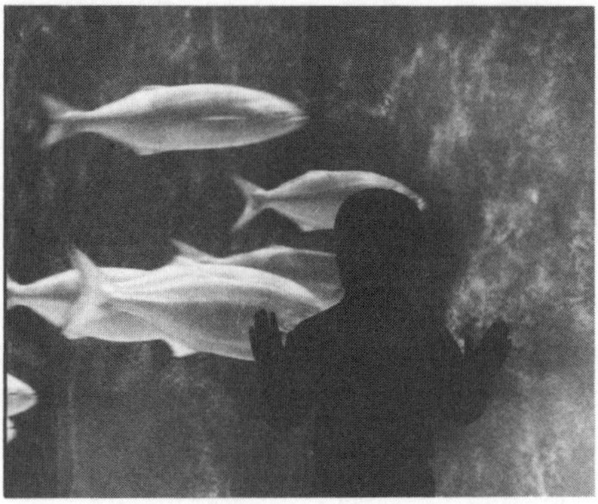

E

song is a series of creaks, groans, squeals, rumbles, chirps, flutters and other vocalizations uttered and repeated in a definite pattern. All members of a population string their sounds together according to the same pattern - producing a "song" distinct from that of other humpback groups - and each year that pattern undergoes minor changes, *changes each whale learns*. Within 23 meters of a singing whale you can hear its song above water, even though the whale is 15 meters below the surface. Humpback arias will also resonate in the hull of a quiet boat considerably distant from the singing whale, an occurrence which set mariners of earlier days to spinning yarns about eerie spirits at sea. Listened to underwater, the vocalizations seem to be coming from a stereo set playing at moderately high volume. If you dive within sight of a singing humpback, your chest wall will vibrate with the strength of its song. Researchers are investigating

the possibility that humpbacks can communicate with each other halfway around the world by singing in a deep layer of water that channels sound for extraordinary distances. With only about 6000 humpbacks left in the world's oceans, they are an endangered species. Fewer than 2000 of them live in the Atlantic.)

A frightened, four-ton whale in a choppy sea is a dangerous companion. One slap from a fluke or a pectoral can knock a diver silly. Dunn had a close call on an initial approach when a flailing pectoral narrowly missed his head as he tried unsuccessfully to cut the line with a knife. The bolt-cutter the Mystic team had brought along was useless, for the line was not steel, as they had been told, but nylon; and so the divers had to improvise by using pruning shears borrowed from a county extension agent who just happened to have them in the trunk of his car. It took the divers, working in shifts more than an hour to free the animal. The lines had inflicted cuts on its tail and side, but the whale appeared strong, and when free at last, it swam vigorously. At first it swam in the wrong direction, back toward shore, which caused the team some anxiety (beached whales sometimes do this and cannot be turned back to sea). But then the humpback turned and headed out to sea. As it departed, it raised one flipper high in the air, as if waving goodbye. Yet it wasn't waving goodbye, Dunn explains, "but just doing what humpbacks normally do. It probably felt good to be able to wave both flippers again."

The type of research we do is easily distinguished from the television variety in which the sun always shines, the animals don't bleed or die, and insight depends only on the talents of a script writer. The juxtaposition confuses and distresses some people, and we receive occasional letters asking us to leave wild animals alone and not take away their dignities by keeping them captive, even animals that will surely die without medical care. This is narcissistic and naive. To prevent acquisition of knowledge obstructs real conservation efforts. Only species matter, and time is running out. What dignity is there in extinction?

28

MMA: Specialties

The Aquarium's Education Department has received a bottlenosed dolphin skeleton from the Department of Mammalogy at the Smithsonian Institution in Washington, DC. The skeleton, which needs to be assembled, was sent here by the Smithsonian in exchange for the bodies of two Commerson's dolphins which we have been preserving in our freezer. The dolphin sent here was reduced to a clean and shining skeleton, not by human hands, but by carrion beetles which the Smithsonian keeps for such work. It took the beetles ten days to complete their work on the trunk and only a few more days to finish with the flippers.

. . .

The familiar winter visitor is Andre, the famous harbor seal which delights summer visitors to Rockport, ME, with a repertoire of cued behaviors. The pinniped celebrity arrived November 16 to take up winter residence with eight other harbor seals and five gray seals

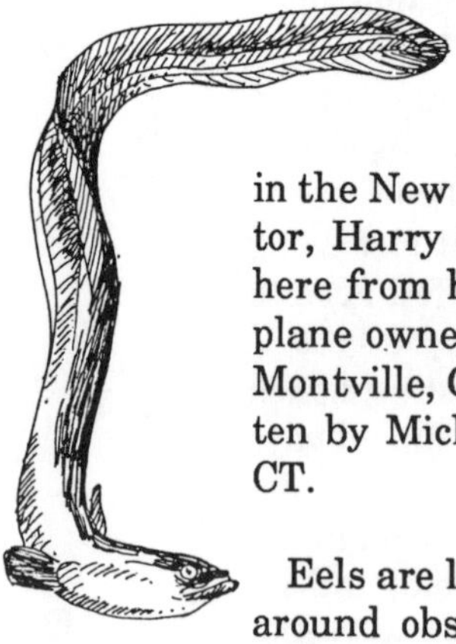

in the New England exhibit. Accompanied by his mentor, Harry Goodridge, the 21-year-old seal was flown here from his summer home in Rockport Harbor in a plane owned by the Robertson Paper Box Company of Montville, CT. The cost of the trip was also underwritten by Michael Law of Chuck's Steak House, Mystic, CT.

. . .

Eels are legendary fish for their ability to get over or around obstructions. They will clamber over falls, dams, logs, mossy rocks and other surfaces provided those are moist. Able to breathe through its skin, a common eel can live out of water for up to 30 hours if kept moist. Anguilla, living in bodies of water without visible inlets and outlets, probably did not get there by slithering great distances over land, but rather by

traveling along underground waterways. One European eel was observed making such a journey for a distance of 31 miles.

. . .

The winter aviary in the Seal Island pond is in place, protecting our birds and their feed from migrating waterfowl. Of particular interest in our bird colony are barnacle geese. Looking something like the common Canada goose, the barnacle goose (*Branta leucopis*) is distinguished by its black breast and whitish flanks. Its call - single-syllable notes run in series - sounds a little like the barking of a dog. This species gets its common name from the Old-World belief that it hatches from barnacles floating on the ocean's surface. An even earlier notion held that the eggs of this bird grew on trees. The breeding grounds of this bird were not discovered until 1921. The barnacle goose lays its eggs on the ledges and hollows of precipitous cliffs in Eastern Greenland.

. . .

The green stuff in a lobster ("tamale") is its liver; the red stuff ("coral" or sometimes "chile") is ovaries. Both are edible and considered a delicacy by connoisseurs. The meat of the large lobsters is not necessarily tougher than the meat of smaller ones. Overcooking makes any lobster meat tough. Chances of finding an "odd-color" lobster are:

Calico - 1 in 100,000
Blue - 1 in 5,000,000
Red - 1 in 20,000,000
Pure White - 1 in 100,000,000

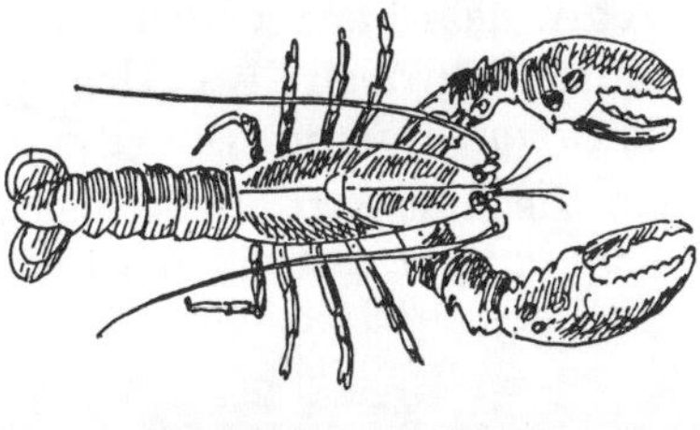

15c

Kids and Squids

Patricia Hagerty worked a transformation of 18 fourth and fifth graders in Newington last week.

They entered the laboratory at John W. Wallace Middle School cringeing and grimacing, and made noises of disgust when they saw the blue-tinged, freshly thawed squid laid out in plastic trays in the lab. Most of them were clearly dreading the squid dissection they were to perform.

But minutes later, the same children were working enthusiastically at their task, carefully cutting into the six-inch squids and searching for the organs Ms. Hagerty identified - the beak, the stomach, the pen, the lens of the eye.

This metamorphosis, from fear and disgust to curiosity, is the essence of teaching for Ms. Hagerty, who created the squid dissection program for Mystic Marinelife Aquarium. "When you know you've gotten their attention, and got them excited about it, that's what keeps me in teaching," she said. Ms. Hagerty is one of four traveling teachers whom the aquarium makes available to schools within 75 miles of Mystic at $50 per class. The squid dissection is one of many classes offered by the aquarium teaching staff, all of which emphasize hands-on participation by the students.

The transformation Ms. Hagerty wrought in Newington was gradual. After seating the children at the lab tables, where each student had a squid, she gave a brief lecture on squid natural history. Then she encouraged the children, most of whom had kept their hands in their laps, to try touching the cold, rubbery squid skin.

Some tried. Sounds like "Eeeuw" filled the room.

"The squid has basically a hollow body," Ms. Hagerty said, holding up a lifeless squid, stuck on her index finger like a puppet.

"Eeeeeeee!"

"They can suck water inside their bodies, and expel it to propel themselves through the water," she said. She described the squid's pen, an internal shell that gives the squid's soft body its shape.

"Imagine this body without it," she said, shaking the limp squid. A girl near her recoiled.

But the children's curiosity was clearly beginning to overcome their squeamishness. By the time Ms. Hagerty began the first part of the dissection - scraping away the squid's outer skin - most of the class was

F

ready to handle the creature.

Some jumped right into the dissection, but others balked when the actual cutting began. Ms. Hagerty first showed the children how to pull out the squid's beak and esophagus, then told them to try doing it on their squids.

"Do we have to pull it out?" a voice said.

"You'd have to pay me a million dollars," said another.

Working with each student individually, however, she got all 18 beaks out, and continued with the eyes, and then with an incision down the middle of the animal. One by one, the children fell under the spell of curiosity and the squid's anatomy, eagerly asking questions and wielding their plastic picnic knives with enthusiasm.

Ms. Hagerty, who has a combined undergraduate degree in biology, theology and philosophy, said the programs always seem to elicit enthusiasm from the children.

. . .

The Aquarium's education program, both at the Aquarium and on the road, has grown since the opening of the Aquarium 15 years ago. Five years ago, 48,500 children had lessons from aquarium personnel in one year. This past year, 65,000 children have been taught.

1d

The Seaport

Mystic Seaport was founded in 1929 by Dr. Charles K. Stillman, Edward E. Bradley and Carl C. Cutler. Through the foresight and generosity of the families historically involved with the land and the commerce of Mystic, and the interest of many friends from far and near, the Seaport has grown from one building and a small collection to more than sixty buildings, ships and formal exhibits on approximately forty acres of land.

The aim of the founders was the preservation of our maritime heritage. To this end Mystic Seaport continues to gather exhibits that represent the industries and craft shops that supported New England shipping, shipbuilding and fisheries.

Mystic, in its time, contributed to the nation's maritime stature in a manner out of all proportion to its size. It is hoped that Mystic Seaport will make a comparable contribution to the knowledge and understanding of modern visitors who come to see the tangible evidences of this remarkable past.

1e

EXHIBITS

SHIPS

CHARLES W. MORGAN 1841 whaling bark
JOSEPH CONRAD 1882 training ship
L.A. DUNTON 1921, Gloucester fishing schooner
S.S. SABINO 1908, coal-fired, steam-powered passenger ferry, seasonal short cruises

PRESERVATION SHIPYARD

Thames Keel Shipbuilding Exhibit: wooden ship construction Visitor's Gallery overlooking main restoration shop

WATERFRONT AND VILLAGE

Australia: ship construction and coasting trade
Bank: 1833, Shipping Office upstairs
Boat Shop: craftsmen building small boats
Buckingham House: 1830's, kitchen garden, fireplace cooking
Burrows House: 1860's, coastal home and garden
Chapel: 1889, non-denominational chapel

Children's Museum: 19th-century toys and activities for children
Cooperage: casks and barrel-making tools
Drug Store: 1870's, pharmacy and doctor's office
Edmondson House: weaving demonstration
Hoop Shop: equipment to make wooden mast hoops
Life-Saving Station: 1874, coastal rescue boat and gear
Lobster Shack: lobster fishing gear
Mystic Press: printing demonstration
Mystic River Scale Model: Mystic between 1850-70
Nautical Instruments: 1870's, instrument repair demonstration
Oyster House: 1874, oyster sorting shop
Oystering Exhibit: boats and oyster fishing gear
Planetarium : shows on navigation and stars
Reading Room: roleplayers from 1876
Rigging Loft: ship rigging gear
Ropewalk: 1824, portion of a ropemaking facility

H

Sail Loft: 1836, sailmaking demonstration
Salmon Shack: ca. 1840, fishing gear storage
School: 1880's, one-room schoolhouse
Shipcarver: woodcarving demonstration
Ship Chandlery: ship supply store
Shipsmith: 1885, iron-working demonstration
Small Boats: catboats and Herreshoff sailing yachts
Stone's Store: 1870's, dry goods and hardware
Thomas Greenman House: 1870's, shipbuilder's family home
Tavern: sailor's tavern (often sea chantying location)
Whaleboat Exhibit: a fully-equipped boat and whaling gear

G

EXHIBIT GALLERIES

Benj. F. Packard : Ship's Cabin from 1883 "Down Easter"
Figureheads: decorative ship carvings
Mallory Buildings: yachting and shipping history
Meeting House: 1850's, film & programs in season
New York Yacht Club Station 10: 1845, yachting, America's Cup
Schaefer Building: changing maritime art exhibits
Small Boats: changing selection from our collection
Stillman Building: "New England & the Sea", scrimshaw, ship models, model restoration shop

RESEARCH AND EDUCATION

1f

The G.W. Blunt White Library, specializing in American maritime history, has one of the most complete collections of its kind. The library contains 350,000 manuscripts, 56,000 ships' plans and charts. Periodicals and microfilm cover such fields as marine engineering, shipbuilding, navigation, marine archaeology, marine law, American naval history, New England mercantile activities, fisheries and polar explorations. Unusual items in the library include a large collection of ships' logbooks, the complete New York Maritime Register and an extensive rare books collection.

Publications. Books published by the Seaport include the distinguished American Maritime Library, a series of authoritative works relating to our maritime heritage; monographs on a variety of maritime subjects and a comprehensive series of catalogs of Seaport collections, beginning with Mystic Seaport Museum Watercraft.

Education. The Seaport offers a variety of special educational programs in maritime history and other fields of maritime interest through the Education Department. School groups may make day trips or overnight stays at the Seaport aboard the square-rigged trainingship *JosephConrad*. Museum teachers will travel to the classroom to give maritime programs tailored to the needs and levels of the students.

The Mariner Program for young people 12 to 20, gives young people exposure to a variety of nautical subjects. Living aboard the ship *Joseph Conrad*, the students learn the fundamentals of sailing, rowing, small boat safety, weather, marlinespike seamanship and aspects of maritime history. Those who have successfully completed the *Joseph Conrad* phase of the program are eligible to go to sea on the 61-foot auxiliary schooner *Brilliant* that makes week-long cruises, giving young people the experience of life aboard a sailing vessel.

Basic sailing courses for adults and children are offered in spring and fall through the Education Department.

Each summer graduate-level courses in American maritime history are offered at Mystic Seaport Museum through the Munson Institute. Designed primarily for secondary school history teachers and graduate students, the courses are accredited by the University of Connecticut.

The Williams College-Mystic Seaport Program in American Maritime Studies is a semester-long undergraduate program consisting of courses in American maritime history, art, literature, oceanography and marine biology. Accredited by Williams, the program is open to students enrolled at Williams College and at 14 other liberal arts colleges.

Muddy Boots

1f

In August 1951, marking the 100th anniversary of the first America's Cup Race, the rudder of the yacht *America* was installed in a suitable shrine in the Yacht Club building and dedicated.

The yacht *America* is to American yachting what the *U.S.S. Constitution* is to American naval history. She brought the attention of the world to American supremacy in the design and racing of yachts and by winning the race around the Isle of Wight in 1851, established what is now known as the America's Cup Series.

Her sailing master was Captain Dick Brown of Old Mystic, Conn., just up the river from here. When that historic race was done and Queen Victoria and her Prince Consort came aboard to inspect the winner, Captain Brown noticed that the Prince's boots were muddy. As the party was about to go below, the meticulous old skipper asked the Prince to wipe his feet. Noticing the astonished look upon his face and the shocked silence that followed his remark, Captain Brown explained, politely but firmly: "I know who you are, Sir, but you must wipe your feet.!"

And That's The Way It Is

45

Sailing back down the Mystic River and following the channel's tricky turns through an expanse of shallow water, I am reminded of the time a boatload of young people sped past us here, its occupants shouting and waving their arms. I waved back a cheery greeting and my faithful mate said, "What do you think they were shouting?"

"Why, 'Hello, Walter,'* I replied.

"No," she said. "They were shouting, 'Low water.'" Such are the pitfalls of fame's egotism.

*Walter Cronkite. Ed.

1f

Pintle and Gudgeon

Just inside the Hogarth doorway [of the Stillman Building wing], as you enter this room, is a piece from the rudder of *H. M. S. Bounty*, mutiny ship of Captain William Bligh. The pintle strap and gudgeon, together, form the hinge upon which the rudder freely swings. When the *Bounty* mutineers found refuge with their ship at Pitcairn Island in 1788, they used part of the ship timbers to build their homes; the rest was burned to destroy all evidence of their crime. The unburnt rudder was brought up after 150 years and this piece brought back by Captain Irving Johnson. An interesting sidelight of the *Bounty* story is that George Parkinson Christian, a descendant of Fletcher Christian, the leader of the mutiny, was for many years second mate on the whaleship *Charles W. Morgan*.

H

Fresh Water

Ice

12

Silas Beebe built [in about 1840] a brick ice house across the road from his home at the head of Beebe Cove. He used it to store ice for his personal use. In 1878 the heirs of Silas Beebe leased the ice house and the dam pond and ice privileges to Hazekiah Wilcox, Jr., John A. Fitch and Elihu Potter. These men started a commercial ice business and used a large scow for carrying 30 or 40 tons of ice out through the cove, under Six Penny Island bridge, and down the channel to furnish ice to the smacks which were bound for Nantucket shoals.

When the temperature fell to below zero for several days the ice was ready. During the days of commercial ice cutting, the lakes and ponds were cleared as soon as the ice was thick enough to hold the horses and sleds that would cart the snow away. With the surface clean the ice froze thicker and faster and no air bubbles formed to cloud the ice and lessen the appeal. Most ice companies tried to get ice so clear that a newspaper could be read through it. Once the ice was cleared by the horses dragging the plow over the ice, incisions for cutting were made. When the surface had been scored in a checkerboard pattern, the sawing began. The blocks were about two feet thick and weighed approximately 250 pounds. It required several people to grip the ice tongs to heft a block from the water and haul it 50 feet up an incline to the wooden icehouse. The ice blocks were stacked in the house and covered with sawdust.

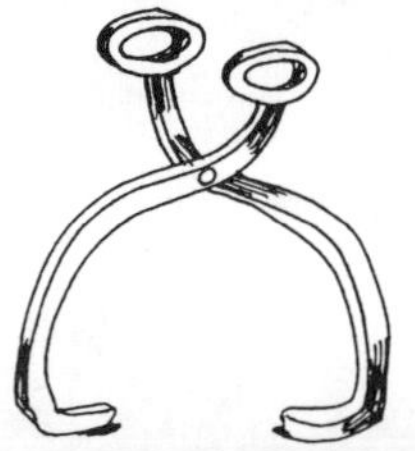

5c

Ice Racing

Lantern Hill Pond and vicinity were again thronged on Saturday with people, there to see the friendly contest between the fast trotters owned hereabouts. There were present of the horses with a record, C. H. Cottrell's bay mare Nellie Mills, Stanton's gray gelding Plough-boy, J. S. Brown's (Westerly) bay gelding Joe Shannon, J. Brown's (Stonington) gray mare White Priest, R. Babcock's roan mare Lady Singular, Hamilton Allen's bay gelding Hamilton Allen. A purse of $20 was to be divided between the best three, in the ratio of $10, $6 and $4. The first money was won by Plough-boy, second by Nellie Mills, third by Joe Shannon.

At the trot on Tuesday Elder Foster's horse Black Prince of New London, Brown's Joe Shannon, Stanton's Plough-boy and Unknown of Providence were the leading horses. The Black Prince led the first time over the course, but was withdrawn on account of a broken shoe, and Plough-boy took first money, Joe Shannon second, and Unknown third. Another trot tomorrow (Friday) p.m.

Enterprise

Cooking Afloat

15d

Mystic Clipper Linguine with Clams

1 cup olive oil
5 cloves garlic
1 can (3 pounds, 3 ounces) chopped clams
1/4 cup flour
One and one-third cups minced parsley
1 1/2 teaspoons salt
1 teaspoon pepper

2 pounds linguine, cooked and drained

Heat olive oil in a pan large enough to hold all ingredients. Press garlic cloves through a press and add to hot oil. Heat should be moderate so garlic doesn't brown and become bitter.

Drain clams reserving juice. Add drained clams with flour, stirring to blend flour. Cook, stirring frequently, for about five minutes.

Stir in about 1 1/2 cups reserved clam juice (more if sauce is too thick). Add parsley. Cook, stirring frequently, until sauce is smooth and flavors are blended nicely. Add salt and pepper. Toss with hot, drained linguine. Makes eight servings, with leftovers.

Note: The three-pound, three ounce can is institutional size. Substitute an equivalent amount of chopped clams from smaller-size cans, if necessary.

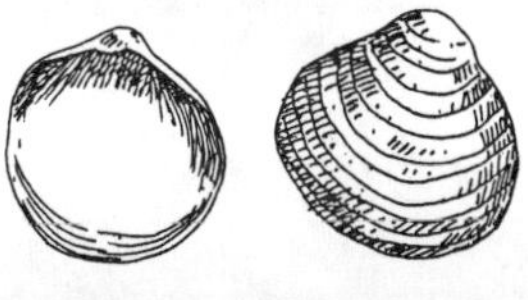

8e Chickens, Ships, Gold, and Soap

The Packer Tar Soap company was founded in 1869 when Daniel Packer of Mystic made a soap containing pine tar derived from the sap of pine trees. This tar had been found to be very effective in treating open wounds during the Civil War and Mr. Packer decided to try marketing it. He took a sample to Edward Allen Olds, a buyer for the John F. Henry Company, a prominent wholesale drug house in New York City. Mr. Olds was immediately interested in selling the soap and within a year the two men agreed that Olds would be responsible for selling the soap and Packer would manufacture it. The company they formed was in operation for more than one hundred years in Mystic.

. . .

At age 15 [Daniel Packer] went to New York to help his oldest brother Eldredge, who ran a poultry market. The following year he went to sea on a packet ship *Emerald*. Later he traveled to Key West with Captain Charles H. Mallory of Mystic and New York. At age 21 he became master of the *Plume* of Mystic, a coastal schooner sailing to Florida and the Tortugas.

. . .

The gold rush fever enticed Packer to California in 1851 where he spent three years mining for gold. While there he began to experiment in manufacturing

C

different soaps. When he returned to Mystic in 1868 he started making "Packer's All Healing Tar Soap." The soap was sold through the Packer Manufacturing Company of New York City, founded in 1872 with Edward A. Olds as president.

Through Mr. Olds sales efforts the business grew steadily year after year. The soap was manufactured for many years on High Street but the building was soon too small for the increasing business, and in 1883 Packer Tar Soap Company moved to larger quarters on Water Street.

. . .

At this time the female factory workers put in a 10 hour day, six day week and were paid under $5 for 60 hours.

. . .

At the time of the Stonington Tricentennial in 1949 E. A. Olds II stated: "Packer products are shipped from Stonington, Connecticut to all parts of the world, and thanks to the foresight of the founders, the well-known Packer's Tar Soap in a metal box, with the Standard of Flags as its trademark, can be purchased in any drug store in the United States and in many foreign countries as well." At that time a bar of soap sold for 25 cents. In the 1960's Cooper Laboratories bought the company and manufactured soap in Mystic for several years until they moved the operation to their home base in Nutley, New Jersey. The soap is still being made and can be bought in local drugstores for [about] $2.75 a bar. Packer's Tar Soap ("pure as the pines") was carried by Mystic ships to remote corners of the globe. The dark color and strong smell endeared it to Pacific natives who refused to purchase any other brand.

Antarctica Found

1d

In 1820, Captain Nathaniel B. Palmer of Stonington discovered the Antarctic continent in the 47-foot sloop *Hero*, built in Mystic by Eldredge Packer.

29

State and Stamp

C

Connecticut passed a resolution favoring independence from Britain on June 14, 1776. On July 4, the 13 colonies adopted the Declaration of Independence. On July 9, 1778, Connecticut ratified the Articles of Confederation, the forerunner of the United States Constitution. The colony became a state on January 9, 1788, when it ratified the U.S. Constitution. Connecticut was the fifth state to join the Union.

5d

The Better Mousetrap?

Our townsman Mr. Edward F. Burrows has originated a device for a postage-stamp, which bids fair to accomplish the desired object of defeating all attempts at counterfeiting. It is a stamp with a coupon - the stamp being gummed, but not the coupon, so that when the letter is deposited in the post-office the coupon can be removed, and this renders the stamp worthless for use the second time. When it is understood that the Government loses annually a million dollars, from the washing and re-using of stamps, and that hitherto it has been impossible to make a defacing ink which cannot be washed out by some chemical process, the value of the invention of Mr. Burrows would seem to be unquestionable, and its adoption by government probable. It is reported that Mr. B. has received an offer of fifty thousand dollars for the patent-right of his invention, but this report lacks confirmation. We hope he may realize a handsome sum from this contrivance, as he has previously hit upon several useful inventions which have not benefited him pecuniarily.

Secret Weapon

14c

[In 1812] Capt. Jeremiah Holmes employed a strange new invention, the torpedo, in an attempt to sink a British warship off the Groton shore.

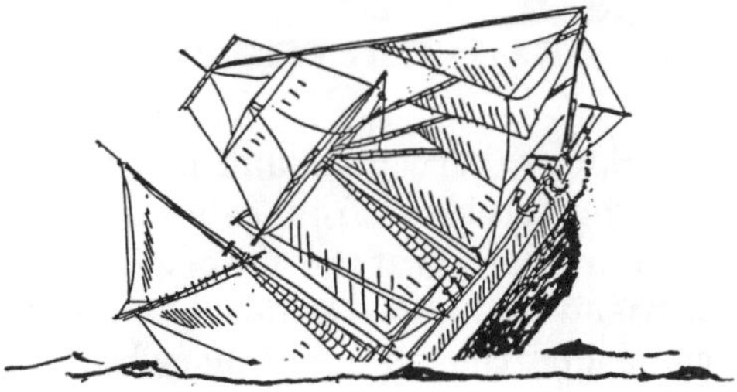

Town and Gown

15e

Books from the Sea

Capt. Elihu Spicer, born in Noank in 1825, went to sea at an early age and rose from cabin boy to master of the 341-ton bark *Fanny* at the age of 22. Later, with his life-long friend and fellow sailor, Charles H. Mallory, he became a partner in the Mallory line of steamers coasting from New York to Galveston, Texas. This made Capt. Spicer a wealthy man.

. . .

Sadly, Spicer's only son, Uriah, died in 1877. In his memory, the captain presented a library to a Brooklyn college. The venture was so successful that he decided to build another library in Mystic to be shared with his native village.

. . .

Plans went forward, but unfortunately Spicer never lived to see his library completed. He died in Brooklyn

Feb. 15, 1893 from an injury caused when his frisky horse overturned his carriage in Mystic three months earlier.

Spicer's will provided for the completion of the building, and it opened formally with ceremonies at 2:30 p.m. Jan. 23, 1894. The villages of Noank, Mystic and Old Mystic were well represented. A large crowd attended to marvel at the beautiful structure.

. . .

It is remarkable that this exceptional Queen Anne Classic Revival building appears today, nearly a century later, just as Capt. Spicer planned it and just as it did at the dedication.

. . .

In the beginning the library was open 12 hours a week. At present it is open 54 hours weekly. There are 5,100 card holders, and although 70 percent of the readers are from Mystic, the library serves 46 communities through the Connecticut system with a projected circulation of 89,000 for 1987.

The Gallery

30

"How did it happen that so many talented artists should be attracted to a quiet, unassuming part of New England?" Many people have asked that question.

The geographical location of Mystic, Connecticut - almost midway between the large cultural centers of the East, New York City and Boston - undoubtedly helped it develop as an art colony of national importance. Fine beaches and cooling breezes from the shore were additional assets. The summer people on Mason's Island, Groton Long Point, Watch Hill,

Misquamicut and Ocean Beach brought visitors from the metropolitan areas, artists as well as appreciators of art.

And then, there was the nature of the area itself. A painter could choose from varied expressions of beauty and life. There was the wide expanse of the sea and abundant inland scenes such as the fishing villages of Noank and Stonington, the Hills of Ledyard, the oak forests of Mason's Island and the characteristic stone walls of the farming country.

The many inlets of cool ocean waters, meeting the warm projecting land peninsulas, created thermal aerial effects with beautiful cloud formations. Picturesque boulders and fascinating rock formations were strewed along the land when glacial action first carved out the coastline.

The setting was one of many moods, demanding attention from artists of tremendous background and reputation, inspiring unknowns and creating a feverish kind of enthusiasm that gave the small,

coastal village a rare and enviable prominence in the art world.

. . .

He was a large man with a warm personality and a closely-cropped beard. And the many artist friends who came to visit and paint with him were the roots of the first art colony here. Henry Ward Ranger, born Jan. 29, 1858, in Syracuse, N.Y., was the first really important artist to become associated with the Mystic River valley.

Today, his work may be found in every major museum in this country. Elected an associate of the National Academy of Design in 1901 and a full academician in 1906, Ranger won numerous impressive honors and medals.

He attended Syracuse University for one year and in 1878 went to New York City. There, becoming an artist who was mainly self-taught, he was known as a water-colorist.

. . .

The present gallery was completed and the first exhibition conducted there in the summer of 1931.

The *Hartford Times* noted on July 25, 1931, that the new gallery was important not only because it offered a suitable and beautiful place for annual exhibits, "but because it is a means of welding the colony together; it makes, of a loosely related group of exhibiting artists drawn together by the charm of Mystic, a permanent organization of property owners in the town, devoted both to sponsoring the best in art and to civic improvement."

The *Christian Science Monitor* hailed the new facility: "Opening of the Mystic Art Association's new gallery on the waterfront of this staid old Connecticut village constitutes an important milestone in the history of American art, emphasizing the growing importance of the exhibitions held by New England's summer artist colonies."

Morgan: 1 Pequots: 0

15f

Morgan Point in Noank is an almost unknown neighborhood in this well-known part of Groton.

It was here on this isolated by-the-sea site that a 1712 lottery began village history.

Jutting out into Mystic River with panoramic views including Long Island and Fishers Island Sound, the picturesque strip of land is considered by some historians as the reason behind the name, Noank. Once called Nawyanque (and other variations) by the Indians, it meant a neck of land, a point, or a peninsula.

The Indian name was used for many years, probably most frequently by the few Pequots who were not among those killed on Pequot Hill in Mystic in 1637. A few who sought refuge in Noank hunted, fished and farmed the land. But, at a lottery, they saw lands and homes they considered their own divided and given to the white men.

Three chiefs complained in a petition filed May 14, 1712, declaring: "Designing men by cunning contrivances, are cheating us out of our just rights."

Historical records show that the first lot was drawn by a man named James Morgan. Morgan's family lived there for 150 years.

It is not surprising that property ownership here is sometimes handed down though families - much as a piece of fine heirloom jewelry. Similarly, it is almost certain to be considered a treasure worth cherishing, certain to increase in value.

Although some residents list their addresses as Lighthouse Point, a decision has been made by the eight resident families, who have formed a property owner's association, to officially name their neighborhood Morgan Point.

The lighthouse home was built in 1868, near the site of another structure built in 1831 for the first light, fed

by whale oil. The latest Morgan Point Lighthouse remains highly visible to boaters - just as it was when it served an original purpose to aid those at sea.

The massive stone structure continues to command attention. It is not, however, easily visible to those on land. It sits at the end of the private main road (which could be considered an extension of Pearl Street) leading into the exclusive properties and homes.

To set a mainsail or foresail.

Before the sail is loosed, let the double block of a tackle be made fast to the weather clue, and the single block be hooked low down upon the chess-tree, and the fall led aft. Then man well the tack and fall at the same time; and when the sail is loosed, ease away the weather-clue garnet let go the bunt-lines and leech-lines, bowse down upon the tackle, and take in the main-tack; the main-tack being down, haul aft the sheet, brace up the yard, and haul the main-bowline.

Leland at Communion

31

Muddie (Grandmother Clift) always went to church every Sunday morning at the Union Baptist church and sat in the same pew, No. 18, unless strangers got there before she did, and then she'd sit elsewhere. Some Sundays we all went with her, my parents, Leland and I.

One Sunday everyone went away and left Leland with Muddie, so she took him to church with her. He'd been before and would look at a picture book and be very quiet. But he'd never stayed for Communion before, so Muddie told us the following about it.

He was very good until they passed the bread to Muddie. Then he said in a loud stage whisper, "What—are you hungry, Muddie?" Everyone near could hear him, so Muddie put her finger over her lips to tell him to hush up. He smiled and settled down in his seat.

Then they gave her the little glass of wine and he whispered louder than before, "Happy days, Muddie!" That was what his father always said when Muddie gave him a glass of her dandelion wine. Everyone heard him and tried not to laugh.

Then at last they passed the contribution plate and once more in that stage whisper he said, "Do you have to pay for your drink, Muddie?"

Beautification

32

1924: On the evening of July 12, 1924, an organization called the Mystic Nature Club was formed by a group of women interested in learning about the natural environment... In spite of informality, they did civic

planting, and held lectures for the education of the public in their lovely gardens, identifying and exchanging plants and seeds. Poems relating to nature were often read, and bouquets were brought and judged at meetings.

1925: On August 5 the name was changed to the Mystic Garden Club. The dues were fifty cents. Tuesday was and has remained the meeting day. There were no by-laws... The sumptuous and bountiful teas and picnics which were held over the years sometimes seemed more important than the gist of the meetings. This caused one old native (man, of course) to describe them as "Gibble, gobble, gabble, git"... With all the fun and frivolity, on October 14 of the first year of the Club's existence, the Baptist Hill ledge was planted. To finance this noble deed, donations were solicited in the village. A whist, cake, and candy sale netted $80.45.

1957: Mrs. Freeman R. Hathaway, Garden Club president, presented her plan for a tremendous civic program of "Planting for the Beautification of Mystic."... The Civic Committee approached the various property owners with the offer of a four-foot dogwood

tree, at half-price; but planted at the expense of the Club by Intrastate Nursery, if they would allow the Club to plant the tree in their front yard. This would carry out the plan of having Allyn Street, Godfrey Street, and Pequot Avenue a double row of dogwoods (one on each side of the street) in full blossom in the Spring. The property owners were delighted with the offer and several ordered extra trees on their own. That spring twenty-eight dogwoods were planted in that area. Three more dogwoods were planted at Fort Rachel Place and Water Street, and two each at several local schools on Arbor Day. The Committee also had seedlings for sale, and 100 were purchased by members and friends. The Garden Club was delighted to receive the Federated Garden Clubs' "Civic Planning and Planting" award for this project.

High Finance

5e

The annual meeting of the Fifth District, Groton, was held Wednesday evening.

We give the following figures from the Committee's report:

School Term last year,	42 weeks
Paid for teachers,	$2,352.50
Incidental expenses,	303.18
Interest on debt,	438.39

Voted, to keep forty weeks for the coming year.

After a free ventilation of various topics connected with the schools, the meeting adjourned.

Litter of '98

10c

Why people persist in throwing papers and other rubbish in the streets has never been disclosed, but the practice is continued year after year in spite of laws and warnings from the authorities. Main Street, Mystic, was covered Saturday with flying papers which, blown by the wind, tended to frighten horses. Burn your papers or throw them into the river and keep the streets clean.

Cure for the sting of Wasps.—It has been found, says the London Mechanic's Magazine, that the best remedy for the sting of the bee and the wasp, is an application of salt moistened with a little water; and even in a case where a person has been stung in the pipe, by accidentally swallowing one in a draught of any kind of liquor, the alarming symptoms that ensue may be almost instantly relieved by swallowing repeated doses of water saturated with salt.

23

Lighting Up

All during the glamorous period known as the "Gay Nineties", Noank streets at night were in total darkness, a condition which was not at all favorable for the many social activities of that time. Persons who were obliged to use the streets at night usually provided themselves with a lantern.

A village improvement society was formed which assumed the responsibility for furnishing some method of lighting the streets and through their efforts, about 25 street lights were installed at strategic points.

These were simply glass cages, supported by iron posts, containing an ordinary kerosene lamp. Every morning the lamp-lighter visited each light, armed with a short step ladder and a can of kerosene oil and a roll of polishing cloth. At night he retraced his steps, lighting each lamp in consecutive order.

It was a task requiring both patience and skill to light one of these lamps when a cold, driving storm was beating upon those frail glass enclosures.

10d

Lighting Down

Mr. Editor:

The failure of the electric lights to illumine our ways in the path of righteousness, last Sunday evening, and your reference to the olden time when there were no such accidents, as vouched for by the late Miss Mary Howe, for the reason that each person took a tallow candle to evening meetings, "and no darkness was their portion unless Parson Hart happened to snuff out the candles accidentally," reminds your scribe that at a

later date this same candle lighting custom prevailed at evening meetings, and when the candles began to flicker and smoke some of the big boys would go around and snuff them out - accidentally (on purpose), and taking advantage of the darkness would kiss the girls. O! those naughty, bad boys; but then, the girls made no complaints. Wonder if any such mean advantage was taken last Sunday night on account of the darkness? If so, who was responsible - the Mystic Electric Light company or the bad boys?

House Calls

5f

NOTICE IS HEREBY GIVEN TO ALL TAX PAYERS in the TOWN of GROTON on levy of 1872, that I will meet them at the following places to receive their taxes viz:

At the office of J. B. Saunders & Co., Groton Bank, on Tuesday, April 15th, from 9 a.m. until 5 p.m.

At the office of Dr. Miner, Noank, Wednesday April 16th, from 8 a.m. until 3 p.m.

At the office of John E. Williams, Mystic River, Thursday April 17th, and at the Store of Yarington & Fish, Thursday, April 24th, from 8 a.m. until 3 p.m.

At Saunders' store, Mystic, Friday, April 18th from 9 a.m. until 2 p.m. At the Post Office, Poquonoc Bridge,

Monday, April 21st, from 9 a.m. until 4 p.m.

At the office of D.A. Daboll, Centre Groton, Tuesday, April 22, from 9 a.m. until 12 m.

Groton, March 18, 1873.

PHILO LITTLE, Collector

RATES OF POSTAGE.

Single Letters.	*Miles.*	*Cts.*
Any distance not exceeding	30	6
Over 30 and not exceeding	80	10
Over 80 do.	150	12 1-2
Over 150 do.	400	18 1-2
Over 400		25

Letters going out of the United States, must be paid for when lodged in the Post Office.

Letters to be sent by mail, should always be directed to the nearest Post-Office, if the person to whom addressed does not reside where there is an office, and the name of the State ought not to be omitted.

8f

Mystic: The Word

In 1614, six years before the Mayflower landed the Pilgrims on Plymouth Rock, Adrian Block, A Dutchman sailing out of New Amsterdam, discovered and mapped the Mystic River. He recorded its Indian name as Sickenames (Siccahames). That name has been lost, and since what was probably a Niantic word spelled as it sounded to Hollanders, even its meaning

is obscure.

The earliest English settlers called this river Mystick which they spelled variously Mistick, Mistic, Mitak, Mistac, Mistuc. As several of these pioneers came from Boston, where the Mystic River was the largest stream entering the harbor, it seems likely they carried over this name.

In 1665 the General Court at Hartford changed the name of Southertown back to Mystic "in memory of that victory God hath pleased to give this people of Connecticut over the Pequot Indians." This has suggested that Mystic might be derived from the English adjective mystic which according to the Oxford Dictionary was at that time defined as "spiritually allegorical or symbolical, 1607, now somewhat rare; pertaining to ancient religious mysteries, occult, 1615, now obsolete."

However, our best authorities agree that the word is of Indian origin, most probably derived from Misstuks-et.

J.H. Trumbull in *The Composition of Indian Geographical Names* (Conn. His. Soc. Collects, Vol. II, 1870) says:

"RIVERS...TUK (Abenaki, Tegwe; Delaware, Ittuk) denotes a river whose waters are driven in waves, by tides or winds. It is found in the names of tidal rivers and estuaries; less frequently in names of broad and deep streams, not affected by tides. With the adjective missi it forms Missituck, now written Mystic."

In his *Indian Names in Connecticut* (1881, page 8) Trumbull adds:

"MISTIKE (Mohegan) modern Mystic River. The name properly belongs to the estuary, missi-tuk, the great tidal river. The 'great river' of Boston bay, which

separates Charlestown from Malden and Chelsea, its estuary receiving the Charles River, has the same name."

Trumbull's derivation is now generally accepted. It should be noted that the final syllable of the present Mistuxet Brook and Mistuxet Avenue is the Indian locative et or us, a place of. This word has numerous variants: Misstucket, Misstucet, Misstucksuck, and others.

All its variants seem to me to prove conclusively that Mystic was originally an Indian word. Its transmission from Boston seems probable. Because the bloody, decisive destruction of the Pequot fort on the west bank of the Mystic opened the whole Stonington area for white settlement it seems quite natural that the river's name should be used for the fight, for the victory, and eventually for the town and the whole valley.

15g

Art in the Streets

Crowds attending the fifth annual Mystic Outdoor Art Festival engulfed this community's streets Saturday and Sunday.

Again the two-day attendance hit the 40,000 mark.

Again about 200 artists, many of them veterans of similar shows from coast to coast, turned the main street into a mile-long outdoor art gallery.

Again they reported Mystic a good market place. "I made more sales here than I did in Greenwich Village." one pro smiled.

Rain hit the show for the first time and caused Friday's opening day to be canceled.

To make up for it the MOAF Committee set up the

show from noon on yesterday [Sunday] as well as all day Saturday.

It turned out to be a highly popular innovation.

Although it seemed impossible after a record-breaking crush Saturday, even more people thronged the sidewalks yesterday in the bright summer sun.

Many of the viewers were business people who

weren't able to make the show in past years. The place was more leisurely yesterday, too, and the festival goers did not have to compete with shoppers and the day-to-day commercial traffic.

The judges had their work cut out for them when it came to naming prize winners.

"The caliber of entries in general this year is extraordinarily high," one said. Even to the uninitiated eye, it

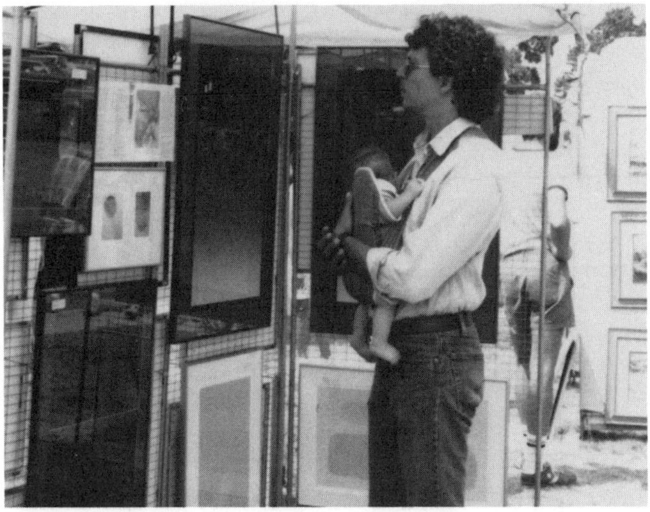

was clear that many of the thousands of paintings were of splendid quality.

A couple of dozen of the show leaders were back for their fourth and fifth years.

A circle of professionals who show at Greenwich Village New York, Pirate's Alley, New Orleans, and at Rockport and other noted art colonies are making Mystic a "must" on their itineraries.

The Mystic Outdoor Art Festival celebrated its 30th anniversary in 1987. Ed.

Water in the Streets

In Holland, housewives sweep down sidewalks with brooms. But in Mystic - where the village is expecting company tomorrow in the neighborhood of 15,000 to 20,000 visitors - they use fire engines.

Tonight for the fifth consecutive year, Mystic firemen will be out hosing down the walks to have them spic & span for the outdoor Art Festival tomorrow.

15 No Water in the Streets

Water Company Scrubs Plans for Hose Down. O.W. Withington, local manager of the privately owned utility would not permit use of hydrants. [They] cannot be used for a purpose other than fire without six hours advance notice [he said]. With the rain today it made little difference.

Structures

Money and Manure

8g

On Old Mystic's Main Street, across from the white Methodist Church, stands a classic Greek Revival building with barred windows, the 1856 home of the Mystic Bank. It seems incongruous to find a bank here, but in the 19th century this village at the head of the river was a busy spot on the lower Boston Post Road; it was in fact the original settlement called Mystic. Hopkinton stagecoaches stopped at the taverns. There were several merchant stores and the community was a thriving center of shipbuilding and cotton manufacturing.

By 1890 these prosperous days had passed and, in spite of vigorous protests by upper village residents, the title of Mystic was awarded to the larger settlement downstream. Until that time Mystic River, or Portersville, had designated the west bank of the river, with Mystic Bridge on the east. Henceforth these would be combined, with a single post office known as Mystic. The village upstream was rechristened Old Mystic and relegated to antiquity.

A

As the original Mystic bustled in the aftermath of the War of 1812, its businessmen took steps to improve banking facilities, for the nearest bank, established in 1822, was at Stonington. The Mystic Bank was chartered by the Connecticut General Assembly in June 1833 with a capital of $50,000.

. . .

The first bank building, constructed of granite blocks, stood on the highway just south of the Enoch Burrows mansion. In 1948 this bank was moved, stone by stone, to Mystic Seaport, where it was carefully reconstructed. At first whimsically called "The Counting House", its true name, Mystic Bank, has now been restored.

. . .

The directors of the Mystic Bank decided to build new quarters... two adjacent tracts were acquired, each for $100 [1856]... a total width of 32 feet extending from the highway west to the edge of [Whitford] Brook.

. . .

The bank sign was taken down January 8, 1889: ex-

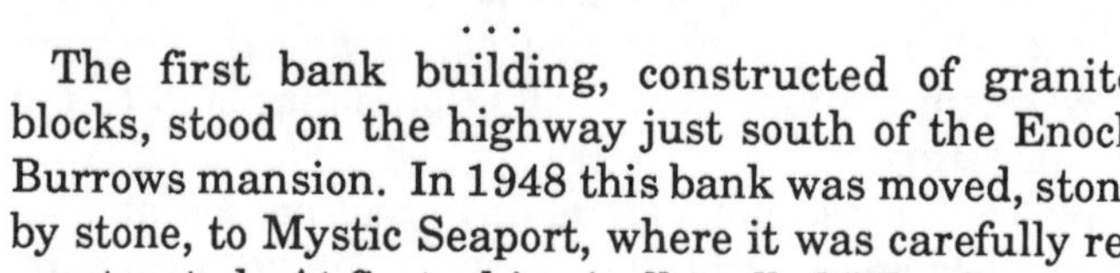

K

penses 20 cents. Articles were sold piecemeal, and the ledger tells what furnishings were in the bank. These included an old desk chair (sold for 10 cents), a lounge ($3.50), seven chairs ($1.75), an old swivel chair (25 cents), spittoon (10 cents)... Other items sold were sealing wax, scissors, tin box, thermometer, punch and "old stuff in the coal room". Also, W. W. French paid 50 cents "for manure in shed".

[In 1965] the building was acquired by a non-profit organization, the Indian and Colonial Research Center, Inc., to house the papers and collections of historian Eva L. Butler. The center pledged to maintain and preserve the building and to make Mrs. Butler's materials available for public use. Today the bank contains a reference library in the fields of local history, anthropology and genealogy, and the wagon shed holds a growing display of Indian artifacts.

Widows' Walks

23

In many seaport towns of New England, houses were so built that a flattened portion of the roof could be used as an outside gallery, and sometimes from these vantage points, hours and even days of anxious watching and waiting were spent in lonely vigil, while the glimmering hope that the familiar outlines of an over-

due ship might even yet appear upon the distant horizon, became fainter and fainter. Because these out-of-door balconies were silent witnesses of many unfortunate events that vitally affected the household, they came to be known as "Widows' Walks."

33 Cutting Corners... and a Ghost

The people who live in these homes represent an elite minority in Connecticut.

There are only 15 of the houses in the whole state, scattered here and there. No town has more than a couple.

They're octagonal houses, those strange-looking eight-sided structures that you just can't help looking at, and wondering about, as you drive by. Why would anyone build one of those things? Why would anyone live in one?

The house was built in the middle of the last century

by Albert G. Stark, a local storekeeper and town judge.

"This is an 1850 house, but it's also very modern" says Cathy Cook.

The octagonal home of Roger and Cathy Cook and their three children is on West Mystic Avenue, on a hill commanding a magnificent view of the Mystic River, Watch Hill, R.I., and Long Island Sound as seen from the house's cupola.

"It's light and it's open. No matter what time of day it is, you get sunlight. And inside, it's open. Rooms aren't closed off from each other. We've entertained a hundred people here and they could all move around."

All of the rooms - 16 of them - have dimensions in multiples of eight. There are eight panes in all of the floor-to-ceiling windows and 16 stairs leading to the second floor. The stairway railing posts and the cupola are octagonal. The outhouse is long gone now, but that, too, had eight sides.

The Cooks bought the house in 1979 and have done mammoth restoration work on it, including installing a new hip roof and another eight-sided cupola.

The Cooks' house and all other octagonal houses, represent a brief vogue in American architecture.

The man responsible for the eight-sided house, which Cathy calls the "only really unique American architecture," was one Orson S. Fowler, a rather unusual fellow himself. He was a phrenologist - a person who believes personality is determined by the shape of the skull - a hypnotist, a believer in water cures, and a generally strange person.

His theory on the octagonal house was that it would make the best use of space because it had virtually no corners and would be healthful because sun and fresh air could come in from all eight sides.

Fowler's theories on houses did find something of a market in the middle of the last century. Within 20 years after his book on octagonal homes, titled Homes for All, was published, about 2,000 of them were built throughout the country.

They have not regretted buying it, Cathy says. "It is a very liveable and contemporary house a century and a half after the octagonals enjoyed their brief architectural time in the sun.

"If we were building a new home today," she says, "there are a lot of things in this house I would include."

There is one thing that she could never buy in a new house that she got for free in the 1850 octagonal: a ghost.

Stark, the Yankee storekeeper who built it, was married to a Southern belle. During the Civil War her brother, a Confederate soldier, was captured and sent as a prisoner of war to an island off Boston. He escaped and made it to his sister's house in Mystic but died there.

The Cooks didn't believe in ghosts when they bought the old octagonal house. They had just moved in, says Cathy, when they began to hear a strange humming sound. "We could not tell where it was coming from, but we kept hearing it."

Someone conversant with the habits of ghosts suggested they try talking to it. One night the family sat up, and Cathy explained something to whoever - or whatever - might be listening.

"I knew this house when I was growing up," she announced. "We love it here, and we're going to stay here. So don't bother us!"

They have never heard the noise again.

18

Noank

About 1900, Noank began to receive summer residents from New York and other urban areas, although to this day vacationers are much less evident than in nearby villages. Partly due to the 1938 hurricane, there are few visible physical remains of the summer visits by business and literary figures. Theodore Dreiser found inspiration in Noank and in his book *Twelve Men* (1919), he described the village as "...a little played-out fishing town." Publisher George Putnam also frequented the town and married Amelia Earhart in the house at 43 Church Street.

...

The shipyards in Noank have been replaced by modern marinas, yet much remains in the village of life in the past century. The town is significant for its architecture because of the concentration of Greek Revival and Gothic - and Eastlake - detailed dwellings which line its narrow streets. Only a few of them date from before 1840 or after 1910, accurately reflecting the

growth of the village in the second half of the last century. A few of the houses have ropeknot bargeboards or wave-like bargeboards on crestings, like that on the porticos of 26 Main Street. The small size of most of the houses, particularly the Greek Revival dwellings with the four-bay facade, may in part be accounted for by the fact that many residents spent much of their time at sea.

Noank offers today, in a relatively small area, an

opportunity to see a wide and imaginative variety of architecture and architectural ornament. The decorative pilasters, bargeboard, peak ornaments, porches and fences, the ecletic borrowing of details, and the concentration of old houses are grouped along narrow, winding streets. A comparable group of buildings can be found in no other area of Connecticut. One is tempted to label these dwellings as "maritime picturesque."

Home is the Sailor 34

All of these, at one time modern and up to date houses and buildings, could not have been built anywhere except, as the writers of the time would phrase it, in a "live" place, and Mystic, Connecticut during the period from 1835 to 1865 was just such a "live" place. Indeed, the village was at its zenith as a maritime community during those years. Six very active ship and boat yards were turning out a score of large vessels each year. In the 1850's the era of the American clipper ship was at its height and Mystic during that decade launched twenty-one ships of this type. In fact, more clipper ships were built at Mystic than any other single community in southern New England. Many other vessels were also built during this period including more prosaic steamboats, fishing smacks and coastal trading brigs, barks and schooners. The shipbuilding boom generated by the government's needs during the Civil War also generated great wealth for many in the community. In

addition, the whaling industry was still very much in evidence as were the numerous vessels engaged in the various fisheries. With the exception of our own time, Mystic was undergoing its greatest period of economic expansion. These prosperous times expressed themselves in numerous ways but pérhaps the most obvious was in the community's architecture.

When visiting these buildings remember that they represent Mystic at the height of its prosperity generated in large measure by maritime industries. Had Mystic prospered later in the nineteenth century there would undoubtedly be more examples of the Queen Anne and shingle styles or had the village bloomed earlier in the century we would see more Federal architecture or perhaps many more Cape Cod and other vernacular styles. But, Mystic was most prosperous during the mid-nineteenth century and consequently its now familiar architecture is representative of the distinctive styles of that thriving period.

Mystic Walking Tour

35

This walking tour is the result of a joint effort of The Mystic Junior Women's Club and the Mystic Chamber of Commerce.

Because of the Bicentennial year, interest in our heritage has been revived and the Chamber wanted to share this with visitors and residents alike. This tour starts at Gravel Street and continues up Clift Street to High and back to West Main Street, and takes about an hour at a leisurely pace.

Those taking the Walking Tour should bear in mind that these beautiful houses are, indeed, homes of people who rightfully demand and deserve their privacy. Observation should be made only from public streets and sidewalks; residential lawns, walkways, gardens, or driveways should be considered as off limits. It is an absolute truth that knocking on doors, entering gates, or peering into windows will be heartily unwelcomed. Ed.

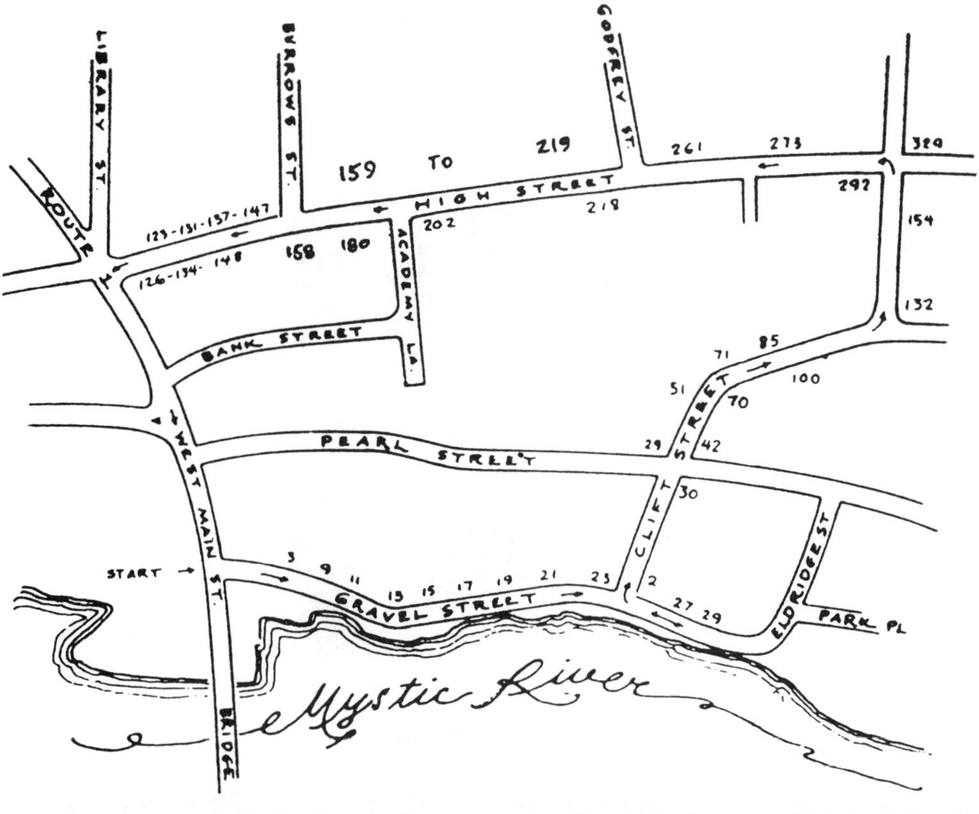

Gravel Street

Originally known as Shore Road, it was actually owned by the adjacent property owners and was not accepted as a town road until the 1850's. The loads of gravel brought in to make it stable gave it its present name. It has always been the home of men who made their living from the sea, which is attested to by the fact that many of the original owners of these homes were sea captains, or at least actively engaged in manning the many sailing ships that were either built in Mystic or called this their home port.

No. 3 - The "Case Bottle House," so-called because its shape resembles the old cases in which bottles of liquor were shipped. Built in 1838 by John Wolfe as a one-family house, it had undergone many additions and alterations through the years until its restoration in 1951. It is now used commercially but retains the look of the original home.

No. 9 - Captain George Wolfe built this typical Cape Cod dwelling in 1818 for his bride. Much the same now, as then, it boasts a huge central chimney that contains three fireplaces. The largest, or kitchen, fireplace has the usual oven as well. The west wing of the house is a much later addition. There is purported to be a resident ghost, but she is old and means no harm and gives no trouble.

No. 11 - This old Cape Cod was built around 1812 by Captain Avery Brown, who commanded the sloop *Minerva* and was bo'sun on the *Hero* in the war of 1812.

The 47-foot sloop *Hero* was built in 1800 at the Packer Shipyard in Mystic. It became famous in the War of 1812 and in 1820 was the vessel in which Nathaniel Palmer of Stonington discovered the Antarctic continent while on a sealing voyage.

No. 13 - Circa 1836 this house by tradition is known as a "spite house," deliberately built into the street in order to block the neighbor's view. Basically a Cape Cod, it has two central chimneys and Greek Revival accents. Originally owned by John Fellows (who must have been the spiteful one), it was later the residence of two Captains Eldredge, both of whom followed the sea in various capacities.

No. 15 - This is a Greek Revival built in 1835 with Italian Villa style additions applied later. It was built by a cabinetmaker, Daniel D. Edgecomb, who made coffins in a basement shop. It was purchased in 1847 by Captain Gurdon Gates, who distinguished himself by making a record run around the Horn in the famous clipper ship *Twilight* and later commanded the steamer *Victor* of the Mallory Line, as well as numerous other vessels.

No. 17 - Henry Holdredge built this house in 1835. However, it is probable that the prominent architectural features - the bracketed bay windows, the pointed gable and the finialed canopy over the door - were added later. The characteristics of the Gothic Revival - scrollwork, finials, crockets, and pointed arches - were easily applied to an existing building. Look closely at the doorway, though, and you will see the original Greek Revival pilasters and cornice of 1835.

No. 19 - The "newest" house on Gravel Street this, in Italian Villa style, was built in 1861 by Captain John A. Williams who made a record run, New York to San Francisco in 89 days, 4 hours, in the clipper ship *Andrew Jackson.*

No. 21 - An elegant Greek Revival built in 1840 by Elisha Denison, this house was also the home of a sea captain. It was acquired in 1854 by Captain Martin Smith who commanded the *Niagara*, the *Simoon*, and the *Selma*.

No. 23 - Another traditional Greek Revival which was built in 1837 by John Gallup. It was extensively added to and changed and has just recently been beautifully restored to its original appearance.

No. 27 - This house is set sideways to the street, perhaps for the convenience of the customers of its owner, Daniel R. Williams, who had a seine business in the basement. At the time that it was built, in 1834, there were no other houses for some way south of it, assuring an unobstructed view down the river. An outbuilding in the rear was a station for the underground railroad. A basement 10 ft. deep, with cupboards and benches, hid the runaway slaves. Matilda Appelman Williams held weekly seances in the front parlor. Note the handsome front door with its leaded glass sidelights.

No. 29 - A true sea captain's home is this handsome Greek Revival built in 1837 for Captain John Appelman, captain of the *Neptune* and the *Hero*. Particularly interesting details of this house are the dentil molding in the pediment and cornice trim and the beautifully paneled entrance door. In recent years the owner was Captain Edward L. Beach, captain of the *U.S.S. Triton* on its historic circumnavigation of the globe underwater and author of *Submarine!*, *Run Silent, Run Deep*, and *Around the World Submerged.*

Clift Street

No. 2 - Col. Amos Clift, a prominent local builder, built this house in 1837 for his brother, Captain Waterman Clift, on land which had belonged to their father, Captain Amos Clift. Waterman Clift commanded the *Atlantic, Plume,* and *Coasting Trader* and was later a harbor pilot in Apalachicola, Florida. This house is typically Greek Revival in the two-story main part, with its cornices and pilasters. The front door is beautifully carved with four panels separated by an oval. The east wing was added in the 1920's.

No. 30 - This house was built by James Gallup in 1855. Note the detail of the dentil molding over the window in the peak.

No. 42 - Amos Clift built this house for another brother, Frederick D. Clift, who was also a builder. Its original Greek revival details have largely disappeared under new siding, but the basic shape remains.

No. 39 Pearl Street - This miniature Greek revival was constructed by Lyman M. Williams in 1850. The trim above the door was possibly added later, as was the bay window on the south side.

No. 51 Clift - Wagonmaker Charles Johnson was the builder of this simple and charming home in 1863. The door seems to be the only adornment.

No. 61 - Ebenezer Marston, stonecutter, sold this land which contained a marble shop and barn to Charles H. Amesbury in 1862. A year later, Mr. Amesbury built this home.

No. 70 - This was John Edgecomb's carriage house in 1880. It was converted to a dwelling in 1933.

No. 71 - This delightful house was Ebenezer Marston's, which he built in 1844. Backed up against the cliff and facing the morning sun, it was secure from the cold northwest winds of winter, as was its neighbor No. 85, also built by Mr. Marston, in 1848. The latter house has been considerably altered and added to in recent years.

No. 100 - This large classic Greek Revival was built by Isaac D. Gates in 1854 on land he received from his aunt and uncle, Thankful and Amos Clift. Captain Gates commanded the *Asa Sawyer*, *Racer*, and *Cremorne*. This particular style of architecture was known as "five over four and a door," referring to the five windows upstairs versus four down with the door in the position of one of the windows. Whereas it was usual to have the door face the street on the narrow

end of the building, this one is on the long side and faces south to the sun and the view.

No. 132 - This property was part of the Clift Homestead Farm and was sold by Col. Amos Clift's sons to their aunt Mrs. Nancy Clift Chesebro in 1879. Whereupon she built this house. She did not live long to enjoy it as she died in 1881, leaving the house to her niece Sarah Clift "for her to have the use of for her life or while unmarried." The original Victorian double front door with its canopy has been removed and a Colonial feeling now dominates the architectural style.

No. 154 - This piece of property was sold by Edmund and Horace Clift in 1876 to Francis B. Mayo for \$130.00. The following year Mr. Mayo erected this house which he and his heirs occupied for the next 70 years. Originally Gothic Revival, it was later simplified and altered.

High Street

No. 329 - Circa 1840 by Jabez Watrous, this was the home of Captain William G. Dewey who commanded fishing smacks *F. A. Brown*, and *Vandalia* prior to living here (1848-1864).

No. 292 - Built in 1855 by Charles E. Davis, this recently restored home was owned by the Donahue family for over 100 years. They were part of the Irish settlement which gave this area the name of "Irish Hill."

No. 273 - Built in 1863 by James C. Lamb, this was the home of Captain Joseph Fred Trimble, Captain of the *Agnes*, *Wm. H. Hughes*. and *G. R. Kelsey*. Basic Greek revival, the porch was added, with its Gothic brackets. The shingle railing must have been an even later addition. This type of shingle decoration was a turn-of-the-century fancy.

No. 261 - This beautiful home, originally the Jonathan Stark homestead, circa 1839, has been covered in new aluminum siding. It is nicely done. The corner posts have been reproduced; the lovely doorway, facing south, has been retained; and the cut stone wall and tree-shaded yard recall the time when this section of town was more farmland than city. It was still within walking distance of shops and ships and neighbors along the hillside.

No. 218 - The next house we come to, across the street again, was built in 1854 by Nathan Chapman who sold it in 1860 to Captain George W. Gates, brother of Captain Gurdon Gates of No. 15 Gravel Street. George was the master of the ship *Twilight*, and the *National Guard*. Here, we see a beautiful cast

iron fence [not here in 1988]. Cast iron fences were popular additions to new or existing houses from about 1860 to 1880. They could be ordered from catalogues in sections suitable to the spaces to be filled and came in a number of patterns.

No. 215-218 - Originally built circa 1809 for Captain Coddington Packer, master of the *Morningstar*, this house has been substantially altered and added to, the northernmost section being the oldest.

No. 209 - This Greek revival was built in 1842 by Reuben S. Chapman, a carpenter who was also one of a group of Mystic men who went to the California gold fields on the *Valentia* in 1849.

No. 205 - This beautiful house was also built by Reuben Chapman, about 1838, and sold to Giles Edwin Lamb in 1866. Mr. Lamb was a merchant who owned the Union Store and Mart on the corner of Bank and West Main streets. Note here the delicate tracings of woodwork decorating the sidelights on the classic front door.

No. 202 - This is circa 1842 built for Captain Charles Wolfe, master of the *Charles Henry*, *Col. T. Shepard*, *Dolphin* and *Gallant*. Not all ships' captains lived on Gravel Street or West Mystic Avenue, there were plenty in other parts of the town as well. So many ships were built here or made Mystic their homeport there was need for many men to command them.

No. 193 - Another Greek revival. This was a very popular style of architecture during this period before the Civil War. Some had variations, as we have noted. This one, circa 1838, has some Victorian additions, notably the acanthus leaf trim in the pilasters around the door, certainly something to set one house apart from the next. Here also is an especially fine cut stone wall, so precisely laid that it required no mortar. The original owner was another ship's captain, William Clift, who commanded the *Hudson*, *Florida* and *Elizabeth*.

No. 192 - The Clift family played a very prominent part in Mystic's history and they had numerous members. Caroline Townsend Clift, daughter of Horace and granddaughter of Amos, commissioned this Victorian home in 1842. A music lover, she had the stair landing constructed to accommodate a chamber orchestra - heard upstairs and down, but not in anybody's way.

No. 181 - Isaac D. Clift, a sailmaker, constructed this house in 1851. It has been extensively altered and has been converted into apartments.

No. 180 - Cape Cod houses were still being built in 1840 despite the popularity of newer styles. This one was for Hezikiah Park.

No. 169 - Originally a plain square house in 1862, the porches and bay windows were added some twenty-five years later. It was built by John S. Heath. Traditionally, this house was painted to match the house on its left.

No. 159 - Built in 1853 by John S. Heath, a shipwright for William E. Wheeler, captain of the barque *Penguin* and the brig *Samson*. The typical simplified Italian villa style is shown in the bracketed veranda with delicate carving. The Georgian moldings in the interior and the design of the cast iron fence are identical to No. 6 West Mystic Avenue. On a clear day, the cupola affords a panoramic view from Rhode Island to Long Island. In the rear the grape arbor (originally arched) led to a plaster-walled outhouse. Under the leafy protection of the arbor, one former owner modestly hung his "long johns" to dry winter and summer. The wife of one owner retired to her rocking chair on her 45th birthday, with the household revolving around her from that day on.

No. 158 - Another early Cape built circa 1829 by Caleb Latham, it was the home of Captain George B. Crary, captain of the *B. F. Hoxie*, *W. H. Brodie* and *Pilgrim*. The *B. F. Hoxie* was built at the West Mystic shipyard of the Maxson & Fish and Co., 1387 tons burthen.

No. 147 - Built circa 1830 by Captain Jeremiah Niles Sawyer who was engaged in costal trade both as a ship owner and as a captain. He commanded the *John Q. Adams, New Orleans, Emeline, Montgomery and Hero*. Captain Sawyer died in 1841 aboard the *Hero* while on a passage from Havana to New Orleans.

No. 148 - A gambrel roof, although typical of the Colonial period, was part of the design of this house built in 1821 by Henry Holdredge. It has remained in the Fish family since 1824. The name NELDIA derives from Nelson and Lydia Fish, the original owners.

No. 137 - Ladies wore hats in those days, and this was Calvin Morgan's hat shop. He also owned the house next door, No. 131.

No. 134 - Amos Tift built his house in 1851. It was the boyhood home of Henry Harding Tift, founder of Tifton, Tift county, Georgia, where members of the family still reside. They still have interest in Mystic, however, being the owners of "Tift House," a Victorian building block on West Main Street. The Tifts also

L

owned No. 126, an early home which has undergone many changes and additions through the years. Built in 1811 by Guy Burrows, one-half of it was owned by Edward Packer, a ferryman on the Mystic River. The Tifts acquired the entire house in 1816.

No. 123 - A Mystic embankment-style house, built on a slope so that the first floor (which was at ground level in the rear) must be reached by a long flight of stairs in the front. The fanciful embellishment of the veranda is a particularly pleasing detail of this home built by Amos Clift for Henry D. Chesebro in 1836.

Union Baptist Church - This imposing edifice was erected beginning in 1861 after the union of several Baptist churches in the area, and by combining two existing church buildings. Throughout the ensuing years additions and alterations were made to the structure until the present design was completed. During the 1938 hurricane, the steeple blew off and it was not replaced until 30 years later when a large bequest from a friend of the church made possible the present fiber glass steeple, with its clocks and the 61 Flemish bell carillon. The 8-foot weathervane is a replica of the weathervane on the steeple of the Old North Church in Boston.

Disaster

10e

Every Silver Lining Has Its Cloud

While the new enterprise committee of the Mystic Board of Trade are looking for industries with which to build up the village, we would call their attention to a matter which has seemingly thus far escaped their notice. Westerly is noted for its granite and it is not superior to the granite quarried from Mystic's hills. Many say that our stone surpasses that of Rhode Island. It is blue granite, free from coloring, will not stain and is easy to work and when cut into monuments, polished and carved, no more handsome pieces can be found.

...

5g Mr. Charles Stanton is quarrying out the granite ledge in rear of his house on Pearl St. He has already got several thousand pavers, and quite a quantity of good building stone. In clearing away to get at the good rock, he has blasted out a considerable quantity of rough stones, of which he shipped a vessel load last week to Race Rock to be used in laying foundation for a light house.

...

A good many startling reports have proceeded from Stanton's ledge first and last, but that one of Tuesday afternoon roused the community like an earthquake, and those who looked in the right direction were able to see the effects of the fearful explosion in the rocks flying high in the air and falling in every direction, but those living or remaining near the quarry were anything but pleased - it was too "scary" for pleasure. A large amount of powder was used in a seam blast, in such a manner as to throw much of the stone dislodged into the air, large and small pieces, with the timber, brush-wood and other covering being thrown in every

direction. A number of large stones were thrown upon houses, some of them doing a good deal of damage. A piece weighing 125 to 150 pounds fell upon the roof of Captain William Morgan's house, on the other side of the road from the quarry yard; breaking through the roof like paper, it carried away the ceiling the whole length of the room, breaking a joist, and landing upon the floor of the South front chamber. A plank was pitched endways through the floor of the piazza, and an immense rock which would pass in loading for half a ton, struck a stone post directly in front of the house, breaking it off like a pipe-stem and burying itself half its size, making a large hole two feet deep in the sidewalk.

Another large stone, weighing probably eighty pounds, came down through the room and ceiling over the upper hall in Mr. Erastus Denison's house, next South of the stone yard, bringing down all the ceiling over the stair-way, the stone bumping like a huge cannon ball down the stairs much to the alarm of Mrs. Denison.

The appearance of everything about the scene of the blast went to show that a much too heavy charge of powder was used.

36

Fire! Fire! Fire! The Hoxies and the Hooks

The roof of the foundry building at the Standard Machine Company was on fire. No alarm was sounded but the Hooks were called to put it out.

Al Noyes, Arthur Lamb and Roscoe K. Burrows arrived at the truck house in the delivery team of J. M. Noyes to draw the jumper to the fire. Al was driving Old Jim. Fred Colby arrived at the same time. Bert Hill was in the truck house, and he joined the party.

The open delivery wagon was backed up near the door, and the jumper pulled from the house.

The jumper, as the rig was called, was a two-wheeled affair with the hose reel in the center. Each wheel was about six feet in diameter. It was towed by a tongue with a rope that extended in front to accommodate the men drawing it. Instead of putting the tongue of the jumper into the body of the wagon, about 10 feet of rope was drawn out, and this tied to the rail on the toe board of the wagon.

Meanwhile Old Jim, the horse, was getting uneasy, caused by the ringing of the gong on the jumper and the excitement of the event. When the start was made, all but Colby got into the wagon and he grabbed the tongue to steer the jumper.

The first sound of the gong as the jumper began to move startled Old Jim, and he made a mad dash to get away. He tore around the corner to West Main Street, running faster at each sound of the gong! Al did his best to hold Jim down, but to no avail. Faster and faster he flew. Colby could not keep up the pace, and let go the tongue.

This left the jumper unguided and a crazy trip ensued down West Main Street. When passing George Tingley's studio, the proprietor rushed down stairs yelling: "Pull in the rope; pull in the rope!"

Jim was now in full gallop, and the jumper was swaying from one side of the street to the other. Ting's order to pull in the rope was useless - it just couldn't be done. Equilibrium was impossible to maintain under such conditions. Having traveled past Kretzer's store, and just rounding the curve into Water Street, the old high wheeled carriage finally capsized, and the left wheel dashed. Nothing dismayed, Old Jim kept going. The tow rope being tied to the rail in front of the wagon, ripped out the toe board, tripped over the seat, and carried away the tail board. Old Jim, being more frightened than every by the crash of the jumper, continued his mad dash down Water Street. Al was now standing in the Wagon, swaying back and forth, and tugging on the reins trying to stop Jim. The fire was reached with no jumper in tow.

By this time the Hoxies had got wind of the still alarm and came running across the bridge, towing their jumper by hand. They went past the broken-down hose reel of the Hooks with much laughter and many boos.

Now the Hooks wanted to get rid of the old two-wheeled affair, and here was the chance. Someone yelled, "Tip her up on the other wheel so we can get the hose off the reel."

H

The entire weight of the hose and carriage was too much for the other wheel and that collapsed with a loud crash. It was possible, however, to unreel the hose, and the Hooks arrived at the fire dragging their hose after them looking like a huge sea serpent playing on the seashore. It was a complete victory for the Hoxies, because they had already put the fire out.

. . .

The Morgan block was afire. It was just after eight

o'clock in the evening. The village was still awake, but stores were closed. A large crowd gathered, awaiting the arrival of the fire companies. Smoke was belching from the windows, and the fire could be seen in the rear of the store on the street floor of the building.

The Hooks arrived first. Bert Thorpe was seen running toward the door of the store, axe in hand. Roughly brushing aside all obstacles in his way, he arrived at the door just ahead of the proprietor. Pushing the storekeeper to one side, not knowing who he was, he went to work chopping out the lock of the door. At first stroke of the axe the glass in the door broke, and all that he needed to have done was to reach in an unlock the lock. He did not think of this but kept on chopping.

The spectators, sensing the comedy of the affair, lent encouragement to Bert by yelling at him: "That-a-boy, Bert. Cut her out!"

The proprietor remonstrated with Bert, and yelled: "Let me unlock the door."

To no avail. He couldn't be heard above the din. So with mighty strokes of the axe the lock was neatly cut out.

The fire was in a pile of sawdust in the rear of the store and was quickly extinguished with a couple of buckets of water. The only damage was to the door, which the store-keeper had tried to unlock but was not allowed to by the over-zealous Bert.

. . .

The Sawyer House on High Street was afire. It looked as if the building was doomed, and the firemen were ordered to take everything out of the house. As the furniture was brought out it was piled up in the yard, a safe distance from the fire. A shout suddenly arose from a second-story window: "Look out below; catch it!" Without further ado, the unknown fireman dropped a good sized mirror, intended for the receiving fireman below. No such luck. The glass fell to the ground with a crash and broke to pieces. As the mirror

landed, John Hoxie, Jr., (it was his first fire after joining the Hooks) was seen emerging from the door, carefully carrying a bedroom chamber nearly full. This John carefully laid away with the rest of the rescued furniture without cracking the chamber or spilling the contents.

. . .

We were at Caleb Burdick's house on Clift street. The fire had been somewhat stubborn, but looked as if it was out. A hole had been cut through the roof to squirt water on the fire. Clarence Shay, then in the retail meat business in Mystic, was on the roof of the house and hollered out, "Shut off the water!"

This was followed by "Hand me up a lantern so I can see if there is any fire under the roof."

Just how effective a lantern is in finding fire was never established.

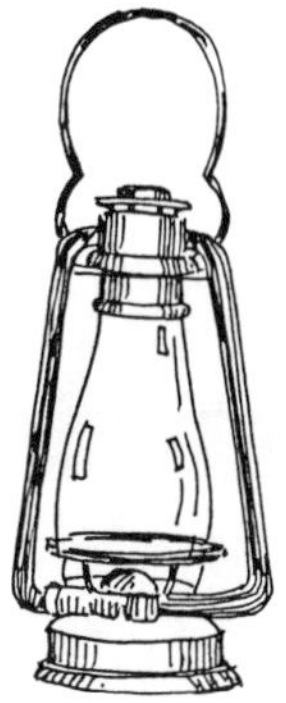

Mystic's Worst Fire

19b

Borne on the winds of winter's first blizzard a fire which burst forth from the Slifkin & Son Hardware Store on East Main Street at about 12:30 a.m. Monday morning rampaged through the heart of downtown Mystic, destroying four business buildings and wiping out nine stores, seven offices and the Strand Theatre before being brought under control by volunteers from 11 fire companies in the area. Left in the wake of the disaster was a loss estimated as high as $500,000. It was the worst fire in the 306 year history of Mystic.

Fire fighting was heavily hampered by smoke so dense that visibility was reduced to zero, by the howling wind, and snow laden air, by frozen hydrants and lowering water pressure, by the danger of falling walls, and the intense heat.

By the early light of morning all that remained were the torn blackened and twisted skeletons of buildings, still obscured by the thick blanket of smoke which poured out of what had once been the stores of Davey News Service, Slifkin & Son, Mystic Pharmacy, Bugbee & Sons, and Mystic Launderette, Mystic Storm Window Company and D'Amico's Barber Shop. On the south side of Main Street, buried under tons of ice and ruins were the remains of the Strand Theatre, Bliss Jewelry and C.T. Noyes. Broken power lines dangled from telephone poles, frozen hose crisscrossed Main and Cottrell Streets and slush and frozen water pumped from the Mystic River during the fire fighting efforts made both Main Street and Cottrell Street impassable until hours after all but the standby firemen had left the scene. As the temperatures continued to drop Tuesday during the day, hitting a low of seven degrees above zero Tuesday night, the water turned into a solidly frozen casket, imprisoning the dead remains of 17 Mystic businesses.

Among the Fire Companies which responded to the call were, in addition to the Mystic B. F. Hoxie Engine Co., and the Hook and Ladder Company, the Westerly fire Department, the Stonington Fire Department, the Old Mystic Fire Department, The Poquonnock Bridge Fire Company, the New London Fire Department, the Pawcatuck Fire Company, Wequetequock Fire Company, Groton Borough, Noank and Submarine Base.

From Ghoulies and Ghosties

Ghost Ship

23

There was a ship to be seen at rare intervals in the home waters. She was not a product of the craftsman's art - nor had she been fashioned by human hands. She always came just as the shades of night were falling. Some of the older people will remember seeing her as she came slowly and majestically through the winding channel into the harbor, not aided by either wind or tide. No word of command was ever issued from the silent lips of that wraith-like figure which stood at the wheel. Just a brief stop, and she was gone, lost to sight in the deepening shadows of the evening. She had come to bring back to the home port the soul of one whose body the sea had claimed.

The Bridegroom

23

Everything was bright and cheerful in the Jefferson Sawyer house that late September evening in the year 1875. The line storms had been unusually severe that fall. Outside a cold, northeast wind was rattling the shutters, and a pelting rain was being driven against the window panes, while occasionally a few drops found their way down the chimney and fell hissing into the open fire which was burning on the hearth. There was within a warm and comfortable atmosphere as the three sisters, Mrs. Sawyer, Mrs. Lucy Wilbur and Miss Lydia Palmer, were making plans for Lydia's approaching marriage, which was to take place later in the year, after the fishing fleet had been laid up for the winter. Suddenly Lydia pointed to the window. There, pressed against the window pane, was the face of her

intended husband, with wide, staring eyes and features plainly stamped with the imprint of death. Even as she pointed, her engagement ring fell from her finger to the floor, broken in two pieces. The following morning brought the sad news of two men who had been washed overboard from the smack *Commodore* and drowned.

23 Out, Out Brief Spot

The big sloop *Manhattan*, Captain Charles W. Davis, was dismasted in a very severe storm in Vineyard Sound. Three men were washed overboard and drowned. Captain Davis alone brought the badly wrecked smack back to Noank under a jury rig. She was hauled out on the North Ways and completely refitted. Nothing remained to be done except painting the underbody below the waterline with copper paint. Roswell Palmer who was superintending the work sent a man with the necessary equipment onto the painting stage. This man worked for a few moments, then put down his brush and walked away. A second man was sent down, but he, too, soon followed the example set by the first man. The third person whom Mr. Palmer sent to finish the work was Thomas Edwards, a man

who enjoyed the respect and confidence of everyone in Noank. Mr. Edwards also spent only a few moments working, and when asked for an explanation, he said that the faces of those three men who were lost in Vineyard Sound were clearly etched upon the planking of the smack, and even heavy coats of paint could not blot them out. Misfortune seemed to follow the old *Manhattan*, for she finally sank on the big flats, where she remained for many years, her timbers plainly exposed at low water, a threat to navigation and a grim reminder of the tragedy in which she had played a leading part.

The Lady in the North Room

15h

Whose is the face of the elderly white-haired woman, wrapped in a black shawl, which overnight guests say they saw at the Red Brook Inn in Old Mystic?

On separate occasions during the last two years, two unacquainted men who stayed overnight at the inn's 1756 Crary House, say they awakened suddenly to glimpse the apparition of an elderly woman.

About a dozen other guests, and the inn's co-owner, Ruth Keyes, say they have felt a presence in one of the bedrooms.

Mysteriously, the incidents are reported only by those who have stayed in the North Room, a quaint upstairs bedroom on the rear side of the red colonial inn at Route 184 and Welles Road.

Passersby cannot help but notice the Crary House, a large center-chimney farmhouse set back from the road, surrounded by pasture, winding drive, stone walls and clusters of trees.

...

Christopher Campbell, a 27-year-old engineer from Canandaigua, N.Y., and his wife, Elizabeth, were guests at the Crary House in June 1985.

"I was asleep when all of a sudden I was awakened," he recalled. "Less than six inches away from my face was another face that shocked the hell out of me. By the time I recognized what I was looking at, it was probably five to 10 seconds before I saw her.

"It was a weird thing, I usually don't go through this. I'm an engineer and everything has to have an explanation. I don't know if it was my imagination, or something triggering me to wake up.

. . .

Albert Clodig and his brother, John, both of Crown Point, Ind., stayed two nights in the North Room. John, a professional organist, was on his way to Manhattan to give a recital at St. Thomas Church. Instead of going directly to New York, they decided to tour Mystic.

Albert, 27, recalls that cold Thursday night. But John, 26, slept through the episode.

During a cold snap in March 1986, the Clodig brothers had requested a fire in the fireplace. While they slept, the room became smoky.

Albert woke up. With only a dim light from the flickering fire, he saw a figure standing in the corner of the room.

"Immediately upon opening my eyes I saw a figure standing there. It was gone within seconds."

"As soon as I woke up, I looked straight in that direction. I saw a woman with white hair, with a dark shawl, just standing in a corner watching us."

Her hands were folded in front of her, he said.

Upon reflection, he said, "I didn't think of it as a ghost, I just thought it belonged."

Clodig called the apparition "a pleasantry."

Campbell called it a "friendly spirit."

. . .

Ms. Keyes says she "felt a presence" in January 1983 before she and her husband, Verne G. Sasek, opened their home as a bed and breakfast.

She and her daughter were unpacking in the North Room when Ms. Keyes became aware of a presence coming up the stairs. She heard no sounds, however. "It kept distracting me, but I didn't say anything. Then my daughter asked, 'Is there somebody in the house?' I hadn't said anything to her."

A few months later, Ms. Keyes and her husband, opened two rooms in the house as a bed and breakfast.

"Right away we started having people ask us, 'Do you have a ghost?'" said Ms. Keyes.

"One fellow from Jamaica took a step in (the room) and stepped back out. He said he could not stay there, there is a presence in there."

Visitors usually describe the apparition as "a gentle older woman," or as a "feeling you're not alone," said Sasek, who does not believe in ghosts and has not felt a presence.

Haunted Cupboard

37

The other night I was telling one of my faithful relative readers about my haunted cupboard. Of course, you don't just lead off with the blank statement that the huge chest cupboard is haunted. The cupboard is in the habit of rapping or knocking so loudly it can be easily mistaken for someone rapping at the door. On a recent evening it gave out with a rather subdued knocking. When my cousin asked if someone was at the door I gave my usual reply at such a time, "Oh, no. That's the haunted cupboard." I defy anyone to let that remark pass without demanding an explanation.

The piece of furniture was purchased for me years ago by my husband. It stands in my dining room, a handsome piece, three drawers above a cupboard with two drawers. On top of the drawers there is a set of several shelves containing most prized dishes. We had had this piece of furniture for about a month or so forty years ago when it started this loud rapping at intervals. One evening we were seated at the supper table when my husband, a Baptist deacon, told me he had heard someone knocking at the kitchen door that afternoon. He called out to the one knocking, told him to

come aboard and no one answered or came in. He was amazed when I told him that no one was there. It was the haunted cupboard.

I am sure that I said this for excitement. The Noank deacons did not believe in haunted cupboards. But I told him I was a firm believer in such a possibility. Since I had made these remarks I thought I might as well continue along the same line by saying it was my sincere belief that the woman who once owned the handsome piece of furniture was now lying uneasy in her grave. Deciding to carry all this a little further, I said if one were to pull out one of the drawers the first owner's name would be written on the side of the drawer. Deacon Morgan rose from the table to put this idea of mine to rest. He demanded to know which drawer. I replied it was the narrow middle drawer. He drew it out and, dear reader, there faintly visible, was a name in pencil, Elizabeth (her last illegible) and these words Died March 15 A.D. 1833!

I swore to Deacon Morgan and I swear to you, my readers, that no one was more startled than I to read the name, for I had no idea there would be a name there - I had said so just to hear myself talk.

Monuments

The Liberty Pole

15i

To the Editor of the Day:

On July 4, the new 117-foot Mystic Liberty Pole will be dedicated. Thanks to the efforts of many people, the project came in under the $50,000 budget.

We ultimately plan to place a handcarved and gilded Liberty Cap atop the pole.

The sum of $10,000 of that budget is reserved to develop a small parcel commemorating those Mystic citizens who have sought to perpetuate liberty in our great country.

$30,000 was budgeted to remove the old pole, provide the concrete foundation, steel base and cap iron, transport the pole to the site and erect it. The committee saved potential costs because of the civic-mindedness of Electric Boat Division of General Dynamics and Thames Valley Steel Corp., which collaborated to produce the impressive rolled-steel base and cap iron; Soneco Services donated concrete for the foundation; Ackerman Lightning Protection and the H.R. Hillery Co., which freely furnished advice and lightning protection materials, the. H.J. Smith Co. which gave anchor bolt caps, and the general contractor, Carlin Contracting Co., Inc., cheerfully provided technical and management skills, labor and materials at cost.

Engineering costs were kept to a minimum thanks to Burton & VanHouten, West Hartford engineers. The cost of the 90-foot western red cedar pole was $1,540 - bottom mast only, the topmast was re-used - plus $700 to get the pole from Willimantic to Mystic.

Not included in the budget is the freight cost to move the pole from Minnesota to Willimantic. At no cost to us, Northeast Utilities made it possible to include our

pole with a rail shipment of their own poles.

Mystic Seaport Museum played an extraordinary role in the whole project. It was the seaport's annual inspection that first detected the pole's deterioration. The expertise and capabilities of the Seaport's Restoration Shipyard were made available for the project - including what is probably the only lathe in the East able to turn a "stick" of this size. In addition, the Seaport turned, fitted, rigged and painted the pole at no cost to the committee. This was a spectacular effort and expended 359 paid staff hours and 128 volunteer hours.

Without the financial support of the community, however, the project would have been impossible. Since 1862 when the first Liberty Pole was raised, Mystic citizens have supported this symbol of freedom.

The Mystic Flag Committee sincerely thanks and salutes all those who have so willingly and enthusiastically helped replace this bit of Mystic's heritage. It's your flag, and you've colored it proud.

William F. Hermann, Jr.
(July 2, 1986)

Highest Art in Town

15j

A refinished topmast and a trio of hand-carved wooden ornaments were hoisted Friday to the top of the 120-foot Mystic Liberty Flagpole at Holmes and East Main Streets.

The new ornaments - an eagle, a liberty cap and a 7-inch sphere - were designed to replicate the original ornaments placed on the pole when it first went up in 1862, said Mystic Flag Committee President William F. Hermann Jr.

Hermann said the Liberty Flagpole was first raised in May 1862 "to spark some patriotic spirit" for the Civil War, which was about a year old then.

The 16-inch liberty cap, which resembles a winter stocking cap, was a popular symbol during the French Revolution in the late 18th century, Hermann said.

"It was used as a symbol of defiance against the crown."

The new ornaments were made by Noank resident Lawrence Anderson, a woodcarver for 50 years, and his son, Gary L. Anderson.

Gary Anderson, 30, said it was difficult waiting for his work to be placed on top of the pole.

As the new ornaments he carved were raised Friday, Anderson, who has a degree in sculpting from the University of Connecticut, said he recalled a statement from a former art teacher.

"I was told my stuff isn't going to go anywhere," Gary Anderson said. "It isn't going anywhere? Hey, it's 126 feet up in the air!"

D

8h

Elm Grove

In nineteenth-century America, a favorite spot for a Sunday afternoon outing was the local cemetery. Mystic residents spent many leisure time hours strolling among the trees and sepulchers in Elm Grove Cemetery, which lies on the east bank of the Mystic River midway between Mystic and Old Mystic.

The cemetery, now 128 years old, contains nearly 9,200 interments and its gravestones read like a Who's Who of Mystic: Hoxie, Grinnell, Greenman, Cottrell, Schofield, Tingley, Spicer, Denison, Mallory.

Part of the rural cemetery movement of the mid-nineteenth century, Elm Grove represents the Victorian approach to eternal rest - a park setting of rolling hills, brooks, and trees, showcasing ornate sepulchers of Egyptian, Greek, and Gothic architecture, decorated with flowers, willow trees, crowns, and trumpeting figures, a stark contrast with the Puritan graveyards of the eighteenth century, whose menacing skulls and crossbones emphasized the finality of death.

The rural cemetery movement began when the American Medical Group suggested that an epidemic of yellow fever that killed 16,000 in New York City in 1822 was caused by an overused graveyard near Trinity church in the heart of the city. Convinced that cemeteries in populated areas posed a health hazard, the expanding towns began to seek tracts of land outside town limits in which to bury their dead.

This nationwide movement replaced the overcrowded town and churchyard sites with large privately owned burial places on the outskirts of town. Influenced by the Victorian view of death as "eternal rest", the term "cemetery", a Greek derivative meaning "to put to sleep" or "a place of rest", quickly replaced "graveyard" and "burial ground" in the American vocabulary.

. . .

By the 1850's the rural, or garden, cemetery had become a symbol of a town's wealth and prosperity. The Victorian era was an age of reform, modernization and romanticism. The rural cemetery blended all three, allowing townspeople to show their civic pride by establishing beautiful and expansive burial grounds.

On Tuesday, July 11, 1854, formal ceremonies dedicating the grounds of the Elm Grove Cemetery Association were held.

Gravesites at Elm Grove were 6 1/4 cents a square

foot for lots fronting on a carriage avenue and 5 cents a square foot for lots fronting on a foot path, and were to be sold on a nondiscriminatory basis.

. . .

A landscaper and horticulturist, [Henry] Schroeder was responsible for many of the unusual trees and shrubs within the cemetery walls, including the weeping copper beeches and weeping white birches.

The longevity of Schroeder's landscaping is evidenced by the many ancient trees adorning the property. The only setback to his handiwork was the 1938 hurricane, which destroyed nearly half of the cemetery's trees.

A 28-Page Salute

15k

The advisory committee of the New London County Historical met in Mystic May 11, 1875, and on that date determined the proper site for a monument to commemorate the tragic 1637 encounter between John Mason's forces and the Pequot Indians. They chose the summit of Pequot Hill.

. . .

Unveiling ceremonies took place Wednesday, June 26, 1889. It was a foggy day, but spirits were undampened. Connecticut's governor Morgan G. Bulkeley attended with the famous governor's Foot Guard resplendent in uniform. Many guests from out of town came, including a number of lineal descendants of Capt. John Mason.

The procession formed near the Mystic railroad station on Broadway after the arrival of the 10:20 a.m. train. The march began at 11:35 headed by Colt's

band. The governor and his staff rode in carriages. Four companies of the Third Regiment, Connecticut National Guard, followed, with the regiment's machine gun platoon headed by the regimental band.

The last division of the parade consisted of commission members, state legislators and invited guests headed by Tubb's band. This contingent filled 27 carriages. Mystic had never seen a better show.

. . .

At the statue, a platform and seats stood ready for dignitaries. Ceremonies started at 12:30 p.m. Charles E. Dyer, chairman of the commission, presented the statue to the state. It was accepted by Governor Bulkeley. After a long oration by Isaac H. Bromley of Boston, 28 printed pages, and an original poem by Thomas S. Collier of New London, those present considered the statue properly dedicated and agreed that John Mason had been well remembered.

Art on the Headstone

In the New England burying grounds of the 17th and 18th centuries stands the only art form produced by a people pledged to abominate all "graven images." Here, in granite, gneiss, slate and sandstone (marble was not widely used until later) is the evidence that the awesome fact of death forced the expression in graven signs and symbols of Puritan emotions too strong to be repressed. Here the very essence of Puritan society and belief is plain to be seen. "Memento Mori" means "Remember Death" not "Remember the Dead." These early stones were intended to instruct the living as much as to commemorate the dead.

The evolution of Puritan theology, as of life, from the harshest and sternest terms to more comfortable forms is seen most dramatically in the development of the ubiquitous winged death's head, the earliest central symbol at the top of the slab. Gradually over the years these stark medieval images were fleshed out and modified to winged mystical heads, frozen in hair-raised astonishment, mild puzzlement, or abstract vacuity, which have been gropingly called "soul effigies" or "glorified souls." Multitudes of these can be seen,

with as many variations as stonecutters. Less fearsome than the death's heads, they are the precursors of the benign, curly heads of winged angels and, later, individual portraits of the deceased. Thus was the "image of death triumphant... slowly eroded away by the superimpositions of symbols of new life." The changes were gradual and the old forms persisted along with the new, but during the eighteenth century the latest fashions in tombstone design spread from the seaboard centers to the frontier settlements. By the 1800's the most formidable symbols had been almost everywhere overcome by the gentle, melancholy sentiments of the universal weeping willow and classical urn.

The shape of the tombstone suggested a doorway, itself a symbol, and was sometimes represented as such with pediment and pilasters. Many and various

were the other reminders of time and death disposed within this frame: coffins, tombs, picks, shovels, scythes, hourglasses, skeletons crowned and uncrowned, snuffed candles, Father Time himself, bats, bones, blighted blossoms, cinerary urns, fallen trees, Adam and Eve falling, and, an unpopular and short-lived fad, naked winged imps of death like perverse Cupids carrying palls or the darts of death.

But amidst the gloom the Christian Scriptures provided an antidote to these pervasive reminders of woe and, increasingly, the emblems of resurrection and hope mingled with and overcame the grimness: skulls and coffins pierced by living plant tendrils or entwined by the mystical vine (the sacraments), hands holding palms extending from clouds, trumpeting angels, trees of life, rising suns, palms of victory, crowns of righteousness, small crosses (considered popish by some), peacocks and cocks, blossoming flowers, fruits and gourds, victory garlands, shells, anchors of hope, doves of peace, evergreens, bunches of grapes, tankards and cups, hearts, open Bibles, moons and stars, bouncing

cherubim, flights to heaven and "saints arising." Not all the motifs, such as the geometric rosettes, spirals and floral patterns have a symbolic meaning and the significance of some forms is still doubtful.

Here and there, on a gravestone which gives January or February as the month of death, the year is inscribed thus: January 1705/6, or February 1734/5.

The year was considered to begin in March,until 1752 when Protestant Great Britain and her American colonies after long resistance, finally adopted Pope Gregory XIII's calendar of 1582, which, among other reforms, brought back the ancient practice of observing New Year's Day on January 1. Some New England stonecutters carved the year in both Old Style and New Style (Gregorian) to make sure that the date of death was clear.

Since early medieval times most Christian European countries began the year on March 25. (One early calendar started the year from noon on February 25.) However, in New England, March 1 seems to have been the accepted day to begin the new year.

Some Days Nothing Goes Right

38

On a beautiful June day in 1883, 18 years after the Civil War, Connecticut G. A. R. veterans turned out peaceably to dedicate a memorial to the honored dead, but marched once more into artillery fire to see their ranks mowed down and their comrades fall beside them.

Civil War monuments are common in New England towns, and the statue in Mystic, Connecticut, is not at all unusual in appearance. At the crossroads of East Main Street and Broadway a uniformed soldier leans on his gun atop a granite pedestal, gazing calmly to the southeast. There is nothing in his bearing to suggest the startling hubbub which accompanied his debut on June 13, 1883, but the chances are that no other memorial had such a dedication.

To begin with, the unveiling was planned for Decoration Day of that year, but had to be postponed when the New England Granite Company of Westerly, Rhode Island, could not deliver the statue in time. Ceremonies were rescheduled for Wednesday, June 13, with the whole county invited. The extra holiday was hailed with enthusiasm. Special trains were arranged, the steamer *Julia* planned a special trip from Westerly, and the Sound steamer *Block Island* announced her first gala excursion of the season from Norwich to Mystic.

The committee of the Grand Army of the Republic of Mystic planned a day-long program beginning with literary exercises at 11 a.m. followed by a parade and luncheon.

Afterwards the men recalled ruefully, "The first advice we received was to spend as little money as possible."

Their plans were completed well in advance. They contacted a host of celebrities and patriots. For a chief orator they engaged the popular Connecticut Senator, General Joseph R. Hawley. Governor Thomas Waller, who lived in New London, also agreed to attend. Neighboring G. A. R. posts promised to be on hand, along with the National Guard, an artillery company from Fort Trumbull, and several marching bands.

June 13 was perfect, weatherwise, and early in the day crowds converged on Mystic by foot, train, and carriage. At 11 a.m. an expectant 2000 waited near the draped monument, gift of the prominent Mallory family in honor of the village's brave men.

General Hawley was already on hand. Everyone loved the former governor, commander of the First Connecticut Regiment at Bull Run and more recently president of the 1876 Centennial Commission.

But then came the first rumor of trouble. Other honored guests did not arrive on schedule. Governor Waller's train was late, and so was the *Block Island* with the Norwich delegation.

The audience stirred uneasily. Their uncomfortable seats had been put together somewhat hastily the afternoon before. Ordered to keep expenses down, Captain Bucklyn had to depend on volunteer labor to construct benches and platform. Although 25 fellow veterans had promised to give him a hand, only two of them showed up when the time came. The discouraged captain assembled some of his students to wield hammer and saw. By suppertime Tuesday, rows of makeshift plank seats surrounded the monument, and a shaky platform stood in front of the pedestal.

And so, just after 11 o'clock the next morning, while the audience waited impatiently, things began to go wrong. A portion of the improvised platform collapsed, depositing several dignitaries on the ground. Fortunately, they didn't have far to fall. But next excitement spread to the audience when a whole row of Bucklyn's seats gave way, spilling a number of spectators onto the soft grass.

Victims picked themselves up and order was restored as the tardy New London train chuffed slowly into Mystic station, just down the street from the monument, bringing the Governor with the National Guard and a band. And while the Governor was escorted up Broadway from the depot, the steamer *Block Island* made port. She docked gingerly at the old wharf below the bridge, the largest vessel to steam up the tortuous channel, but she carried nearly 1000 excursionists and 150 Norwich Grand Army boys in their best uniforms.

To martial drumbeat, the visiting troops disembarked and, preceded by their Mystic escort, started for the ceremonies. Stepping smartly down Front Street they made a right turn into East Main. The monument was almost in sight. Passing Willow Street, the first intersection, they could see the waiting crowds.

At the next corner, Jackson Avenue, Officer of the Day Bucklyn had stationed the Fort Trumbull artillery battery, ready to fire a 38-gun salute, one for each state in the Union, when the monument was unveiled. The guns were on the east side of the street, muzzles pointing westward toward the bridge and the advancing troops. Instructions were to fire when the speeches were over, and all hands were forming the parade a safe distance beyond the monument.

But during the awkward pause as belated guests assembled, the artillery officer, Lieutenant Fish, thought it would be appropriate and diverting to fire a salute in honor of Governor Waller.

Thus it happened that Fish gave the order to fire this salute at the exact moment the Mystic veterans were passing Jackson Avenue, happily escorting the Norwich troops to places of honor. The procession was not more than 20 feet from the gun muzzles when the opening shot was fired.

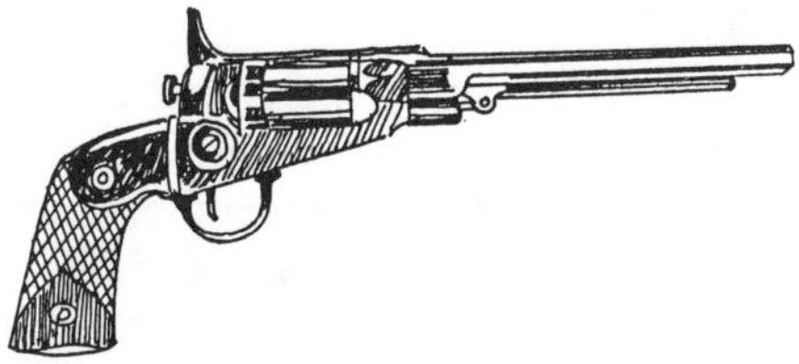

The first discharge of powder poured into the Mystic platoon. As the men fell away in confusion, their Norwich comrades bore the brunt of the second shot. Fortunately, the artillery refrained from firing a third time.

It was Bull Run all over again. Twenty-eight men were felled, struck by coarse grains of powder, their clothing torn and scorched. Some were marked and scarred by powder burns, others hit with pieces of wadding. There were no fatalities, but several required medical attention, including three Norwich visitors. Captain J. C. Brewer was badly cut and burned about face, legs, and body. Lieutenant Carruthers, assistant postmaster at Norwich, suffered a concussion and an eye injury from a heavy charge of powder in the face. Charles Young bled profusely from a severed leg artery.

Three Mystic men, Captain Henry Latham, Warren Burnett and Frank Cleveland, were wounded about the face. But of the hosts, Captain Robert Palmer Wilbur was the worst hurt. The well-known shipmaster, just retired from the sea, had commanded ships *Dauntless* and *M.P. Grace*, but never met such rough treatment on the ocean.

The first blast cut Captain Wilbur's face; grains of powder ignited his shirt. Then a piece of gun wad penetrated his pants' leg, set his canton flannel underdrawers afire, and raised a large blister under his knee. In his vest pocket the captain carried a fine gold watch presented to him by Queen Victoria's government for his rescue of 80 officers and men from

a sinking British ship. A large fragment of waste struck the Captain's chest, hitting the watch with such force that the gold case was badly dented. The hands stopped at 11:26. Captain Wilbur always believed the watch saved his life.

Yet in spite of the accident, the dedication went on. The program proceeded as planned, punctuated at intervals by collapsing of platform and seats which continued to break until they were a perfect wreck.

After the literary exercises, the monument was unveiled at last, and without benefit of the 38-gun salute! Then the parade wended down East Main, crossing the bridge over Mystic River to West Main Street, around the block, and over the bridge again. The crowd wound up at Jackson Avenue, happily this time, for there, in a 140-foot tent, lunch was served to 1300 marchers and guests. Mystic women had prepared lobster, baked beans, piles of ham and tongue sandwiches, and an assortment of cakes for dessert. At each of the 1300 places was a buttonhole bouquet. Using steam from Mr. Morgan's nearby machine shop, the ladies brewed eight barrels of delicious coffee. The lavish luncheon was easily the most pleasant chapter of the dedication.

At 4 p.m. a sudden shower broke and everyone scrambled for home or shelter, bringing the Dedication Day to a fitting close.

H

Recreation

Camping in the Pribilofs

28

The young man appeared suddenly at the top of the grassy rise next to the Pribilof exhibit, startling the attendant who was tidying up her station in anticipation of the first visitors of an already warm summer morning.

"Hi," he said, stepping from the heavy marsh grass onto the sidewalk that rims Seal Island. The young woman was too flabbergasted to reply. Where had this guy come from? The 14 acres of scrub and tall grass on the other side of the rise were fenced in - no way to enter there. Nor had he come through the main entrance: the Aquarium would not open for another five minutes. As the strange visitor headed toward the boardwalk over the duck pond, the attendant hurried to the top of the rise, sensing that the key to this mystery might lie beyond it. She was right. In a hollow not far below was a red nylon tent, its green tongue of a sleeping bag lolling out. He had camped there overnight!

Coming out of the men's room, smiling, refreshed, his long hair wet and combed back, the secret camper was confronted with his trespassing. He cheerfully admitted his transgression. "Oh, sure, it's a really neat place. I've been out there for two nights," he said.

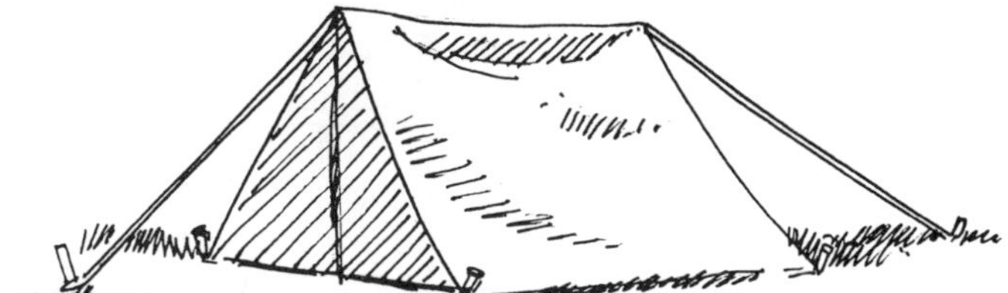

151 Peace... and bring your own hatchet

Tranquillity rules today in the name of peace over a chunk of hillside woodland along the Mystic River.

Tranquillity, in theory and practice, long has hovered over the spot where, year after year, thousands tenaciously fought a battle against war, and young ladies in Grecian robes later danced lightly around a lotus pond.

But long gone are the hot August rallies of the Universal Peace Union. Gone are the genteel squeals of the daughters of the wealthy as they gamboled at Camp Mystic.

Here in perpetuity is the Peace Sanctuary Nature Preserve. Ten acres or so of trees and trails bordering River Road, land once passed by the Pequot Indians to white settlers and now maintained by the Thames Science Center.

A century ago, when the tree line was much farther up the hill, thousands would troop each summer to what had been known as Fish's Grove to hear the

Peace Meeting Doves denounce war, the Ku Klux Klan, lynching and racial prejudice. They would lend full-bodied support to the cause of women's suffrage and better treatment of the Indians.

August rallies of the Universal Peace Union, created by Quakers and reformers in May 1866, became family outings for local residents. Gatherings on the hill, for all the intensity of the Doves, took on the air of country fairs, replete with parasols, peddlers and vendors.

After meeting at Fish's Grove for years, the trustees of the Universal Peace Union bought the 10 acres from members of the Fish family for $400 in March 1890. Six years later, they dedicated their Peace Temple, a 50-foot by 80-foot, open-sided auditorium, built on the hill.

The fervor behind the Peace Union began to wane about the time of the Spanish-American War. With the nation at war, the Doves' attacks on the government and soldiers found few listeners.

By 1906, peace meetings in Mystic weren't selling any more and the Universal Peace Union considered selling the grounds.

. . .

Born in 1886 in Tappan, Ohio, Mary L. Jobe had made several climbing expeditions in the Canadian Rockies. Her maps of unknown territory there led the Geographic board of Canada to name Mt. Mary Jobe in her honor.

In 1914 Miss Jobe purchased the Peace Grove. In 1924, she would marry a noted African explorer named Carl Akeley and make an expedition to Africa with him two years later.

But beginning in 1916, she concentrated on her camp for well-bred girls.

The fee for the season was $375, and advertisements appeared in such magazines as *Vogue*. Eighty or more girls, many from well-to-do suburbs of New York, would swim in the Mystic River, climb through rocky areas, ride horseback and journey from Long Island Sound to Mystic Island in a 65-foot launch, the *Northern Light*.

Girls would participate in plays, masquerades and circuses, and also aesthetic dancing in Grecian robes.

Noted explorers, poets, and naturalists would be among the speakers Mary L. Jobe invited to come to the camp. She would entice them with the idea of a weekend in the country and a directive to bring a hatchet to cut firewood.

Camp Mystic began to wane after Carl Akeley died on the couple's 1926 expedition in Africa. The Depression also hurt attendance. Mrs. Akeley closed the camp after the 1930 season.

Pequotsepos Wildlife Sanctuary

39

This sanctuary offers you the recreation of a quiet walk to observe wildlife. Over 150 species of birds have been observed here as well as ferns, reptiles and amphibians, and wildflowers. On the more than 4 miles of trails you will find a variety of habitats, ponds, swamps, rustic bridges, and so forth. An old quarry, a man-made duckpond, and areas left in an unmanaged state as well as managed areas, creating a balance and comparison of the two areas may be observed. The

Trailside Interpretive Museum contains exhibits, both live and mounted, in an attempt to interpret the outdoor classroom, the sanctuary, for the more than 30,000 visitors annually.

More than 10,000 school children visit the nature center annually for natural history and environmental science classes. Programs are varied for all ages, from 3 years old to adults.

In 1943 the Mystic Garden club approached the Denison Society, a family organization, with the suggestion that a wildlife sanctuary be created on some of its land. The Denison Society agreed, provided that a satisfactory organization could be found to administer it. The Pequot Sepos Wildlife Sanctuary, Inc., came into being and rented the land for one dollar a year for 25 years, with a renewal option. Devoted leadership and generous giving of funds, time and various talents have brought it to its present condition.

"Pequot sepos" comes from the name of the Indian tribe that lived here and "sepos" meaning "brook," hence, this is the Pequots' brook.

Ram-Goat/Ram/Bradford's/ Mystic Island

8j

Mystic Island has a colorful past that belies its tranquil appearance today. Lying between Mason's Island and the town of Noank, Connecticut at the mouth of the Mystic River, it is now the site of a private home. But a look into its past reveals a great variety of activities: an illegal championship prize fight, fiercely competitive sailboat races, a girls camping site, and a lavish resort hotel and recreation spot that attracted vacationers from all over southeastern Connecticut in the 1800's. [1]

. . .

And so Mystic Island enters a new and more private phase of its history. Gone is the African slave cutting wood, gone too are the hordes of vacationers summer-

ing at the Nauyaung House or Mystic Island Hotel. No more prize fights [2] or dedicated sailors racing across the Sound. No more girl campers in white middy blouses and navy blue serge bloomers struggling with the mosquitoes. No more transient sailors spending the night at a comfortable boatel. Just the Canada geese resting on their way north, or a pair of blue heron standing on a rock by the beach, or the laughter of little children and the barking of dogs as they run after the sheep on Mystic Island.

[1] Also in the late 1700's a smallpox hospital.
[2] Billy Edwards of New York beat Sam Collyer of Baltimore for the lightweight championship of America in 41 rounds.
Ed.

Miscellany

Backing and Filling

7

Before steam-tugs were so plentiful, vessels relied upon the tides, in many instances, to get them to sea.

You may drift a vessel down broadside to the current, keeping the yards counter-braced as in lying-to, shooting ahead, or backing astern to avoid danger; then, as you approach either shore, you may fill away until she gathers sufficient headway for stays, or wear around, putting her head towards the other shore; this is termed backing and filling.

Reward

5c

The village was thrown into the greatest confusion, Friday, by the frantic appearance of our friend and neighbor, Mr. Morgan, who wildly rushed from store to store, posting notices, and offering twenty-five dollars reward for the recovery of a lost diamond pin which had been loaned him by a friend, and was considered very valuable. The day was spent in anxious solicitude and eager expectancy by our friend M., who feared that he had gazed upon his 'bosom' companion for the last time. But all trouble must have an end and Saturday morning, as Mr. Ferguson of Norwich (who is now stopping in Mystic) was leading his horse from the barn where it had been kept for a few days, his eye caught the glitter of the precious stone upon the floor, and quickly he secured it, and with it hastened to the nearest store, where it was exchanged for the reward. Just before its recovery, Mr. M. had waited upon the real owner of the pin, who offered to settle for one dollar and seventy-five cents, the original cost of the pin! But it was too late to take down his papers, and he had to suffer the consequences.

5

10

All The News That Fits We Print (or What's *Really* Important)

13

Charles C. Brightman of West Mystic has been granted an original pension of $6 per month.

A tally-ho coach passed through town Saturday advertising a bicycle lamp.

John W. DeVean, who was struck by a fast freight recently at Baker's bridge, has recovered sufficiently to permit his walking out. His many friends are glad to see him again.

The kissing bug has appeared in Mystic and several handsome specimens of this queer member of the insect kingdom have been caught by residents of the valley. Owen Lamb, James E. F. Brown and John G. Clift have caught exceptionally large ones.

A telephone has been placed in C. Q. Eldredge's house near Old Mystic.

T. P. McNinney of New York was a guest of G. A. Perkins over Sunday. Mr. McNinney is a horseman of note and owns a cattle ranch in South Dakota.

Miss F. Marguerite Foote has resigned her position as a teacher in the Broadway schools, and her place is desired by many applicants.

The Stonington nine will play the Riverside Wheelmen team on the Walnut Grove Diamond to-morrow afternoon. A good game is promised and it is hoped there will be a large attendance. Ladies are admitted to the grounds free.

Having nothing else to do one evening recently, two borough gentlemen endeavored to count the number of borough residents who answered to the name of "Charles." Seventy-one was the result of their labors, and even then they were not sure that all of that name had been included in the count.

Mr. John G. Clift has brought a new horse for his truck. He's a full horse, and no discount.

The statement of Capt. Brown of Noank concerning an abundance of seals on Fishers Island is corroborated by the observation of Capt. John Washington, who one day last week counted seventeen in the same locality.

That sale of Toilet Sets at the Bazar is not of old shop-worn things but new and up-to-date decorations and shapes.

Mrs. Nelson Lamb, who resides on Ashbey street, Mystic, visited the business portion of the town Wednesday for the first time in four years.

Licensed beer wrought out its legitimate fruits in a street brawl and fight in the vicinity of Mrs. Mabbett's on Saturday night last. One or more chaps from the upper village are said to have had a lively hand in the melee. In the language of the late Mrs. Swisbelm, or somebody else: "They fought, they milled, and plenty of dirty claret they spilled; but, sad to relate, nobody was killed."

There was no ball game Saturday on account of the rain.

The cherry crop has been quite large this year but it is now exhausted.

Mrs. Freelove Watrous of Hope Valley is visiting friends in town.

A night blooming cereus with several exquisite blossoms was on exhibition in the bow window of Mrs. Moses A. Pendleton's residence in the borough Saturday and Sunday evenings. Many admired the beautiful flowers.*

---

*Flowers open in night and produce remarkable effect because of their beauty and fragrance. Some species are reported to have medicinal value, but beauty and fragrance of flowers should have a therapeutic effect on most confirmed of pessimists. Not surprising that flowering time is announced in newspapers. A plant that can be grown in a 10-in. pot and produce flowers that may be 15 in. across is bound to hold interest of almost anyone. 43

Mystic's Fourth Estate 46

Mystic had several newspapers prior to the Civil War but none of them lasted longer than a few years. The *Pioneer* was started by Amos Watrous in 1859, and succeeded in 1870 by the *Mystic Journal*, edited by Walter Miner. In 1873 Lucius Guernsey published the *Mystic Press*. In 1870 Jerome Anderson started the *Stonington Mirror* in the Borough which consolidated with the *Journal* and outlasted the *Press* so that by 1901 it was the only local paper in the area. The *Mirror* was continued by his son and grandson until 1954.

8a

Milestones

1816 The famous Freezing Year during which snow fell everymonth throughout New England; crops much damaged; food prices soared.

1895 Southern New England Telephone Co. installed service to 30 houses in Mystic at $18 per subscriber.

1902 Feb. 11 - *Jennie R. DuBois*, 5-masted, 2,227-ton schooner, built at Holmes Shipyard, West Mystic, for Sutton fleet; cost $100,000; largest ever built on New England coast; 100 mensteadily employed since keel laid last April.

1906 Jan. 20 - prices advertised: lard, 5 lb. 40c; canned peas, 10c; canned tomatoes, 3 for 25c; pk. kale, 20c; pk. spinach, 25c; cabbage, 2c; potatoes, 90c bu.; navel oranges, 20c doz.; Fla. oranges, 30c doz.

1908 Aug. 31 - Richard Hoben, 7 yrs., 1st automobile accident victim in Mystic - he darted before car of John Dixie, Phila. only slightly injured; driver blameless since car moving less than 7 m.p.h.

1908 Louis Doyle's garage opened in Mystic, and May 8 the *Mirrorr* advertised: "Jackson Automobiles, Model H, 35 h.p., 41/2 x 4 1/2 motor, 32 x 4 tires, 110 x 12. in. wheel base;multiple disc clutch and selective type transmission; equipment includes magneto, lights, etc. Mystic Auto Station, Mystic."

1913 Feb. 15 - Harry M. Jones, aviator who left Boston for New York a month ago, mistook the Mystic for the Thames and landed in Wm. R. Fish's lot at West Mystic. Hundreds went to see the plane, 1st in this vicinity.

1920 Average local earnings: Machinists, brick-layers, plumbers, $1800-2000 yr.; blacksmiths, print-ers, glaziers, $1500-1800; hod carriers, $1200-1400; highschool teachers,$1100; elementary school teach-ers, $800.

1928 Aug. - Mystic River yielded plentiful supply of blue shellcrabs, but older residents still recall when Capt. Jesse Crary brought the 1st from Charleston, South Carolina, and liberated them inriver.

1926

THIS IS TO ANNOUNCE
the appointment of

John Carlson

Elm Street, Stonington

As Local Dealer
for the

PONTIAC and OAKLAND MOTOR CARS

PONTIAC		OAKLAND	
Coach	$910	Coach	$1,195
Coupe	910	Landau Coupe	1,325
		Standard Sedan	1,295
		Landau Sedan	1,395

Delivered at your door.

62 Years Later

Mystic's Brustolon Buick - Pontiac offers the 1988 Pontiac Grand Prix, Motor Trend car of the year, for $12,539.

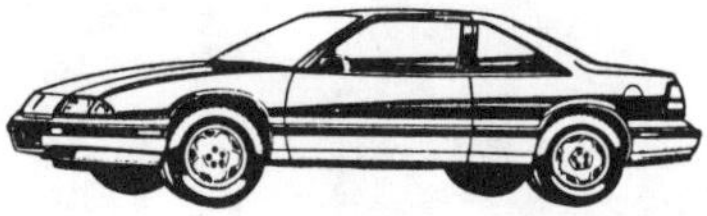

Jumping out of Gigs.—Should it be necessary, in consequence of the horse's running away, or any other cause, *when riding in a gig*, to quit it hastily—if it be possible, *leap out behind*, taking care not to lean too forward, which is by far the safest method ; for the motion of the carriage being opposite to the direction of the leap, the person will come to the ground with the least possible force.

H

We think our town
is Heaven
Please dont drive
like Hell
through it!

G

Guest of the Village

42

I had to submit to the customary & exasperating drive around town in a freezing open buggy this morning to see the wonders of the village. They always consist of the mayor's house; the ex-mayor's house; the house of a State Senator; house of an ex-governor; house of a former member of Congress; the public school with its infernal architecture; the female seminary; paper mill or factory of some kind or other; the cemetery; the court house; the plaza; the place where the park is going to be - & I must sit & shiver & stare at a melancholy grove of skeleton trees & listen while my friend gushes enthusiastic statistics & dimensions. All towns are alike - all have the same stupid trivialities to show, & all demand an impossible interest at the suffering stranger's hands. Why won't these insane persecutors believe me when I protest pleadingly that I don't care two cents for all the thrilling wonders the village can boast.

How I gloat in secret when one of these people regrets that I cannot 'remain over' & see his accursed village! And how unblushingly I repeat the threadbare lie that I am sorry!

After the natural wonders are all visited, then we have to call on other inanimated wonders with dull faces, but with legs to them that show them to be human: the mayor; the richest man; the wag of the village (who instantly assails me with old stale jokes and humorous profanity); the village editor - & a lot more of people I take no possible interest in & don't want to see. And when by some divine accident one of them isn't at home what a fervent prayer of thankfulness rises up in my heart!

- In a letter from Samuel Clemens (Mark Twain) to his fiancee, Olivia Langdon, November 15, 1869.

I

Afternotes

• The length of the Mystic River varies according to which text is read. The editor assayed its length by driving from Morgan Point to Old Mystic on the west shore and subtracting the east-west doglegs. Answer: 6.0 miles.

• It cannot be proved that early Dutch explorer Adrian Block was a forebear of H&R, but each in his time has contributed to security in the valley.

• It is best to understand that the Bingeing item and those items in All The News... were written at a time when fine writing (and honed humor) and a full appreciation of readership were in style. The 'good old days'?

• We must 'fess up. The sign on page 110 exists, with its confusing message, at the Noank pumping station. We spoofed the sign on page 111; that sign exists not at all except for purposes of taking the picture.

• Here is the translation from the Latin on page 63:

> He, who would keep himself busy, let him equip these two things: a ship and a woman. For no two things involve more business once you start to fit them out. Nor are these two things ever sufficiently adorned, nor is any excess of adornment enough for them.
>
> -- Plautus, 200 B.C.